CREATING CONSENSUS

THE JOURNEY TO BANNING CLUSTER MUNITIONS

GEETANJALI MUKHERJEE

CONTENTS

To the victims and survivors, and the members of the Cluster Munition Coalition, whose courage and determination to transform their vision into a reality is an inspiration to all.

INTRODUCTION

This treaty has not come about because it was the mainstream, natural thing to do. It has come about because individual human beings decided together
to fight against something, to struggle against a constant injustice and to overcome it...
– Thomas Nash, Oslo Signing Conference

Three young boys were playing in a field, when they came across what looked like a small metal ball. They started kicking it around, and a few minutes later, the ball exploded. One boy died instantly, while the others had major injuries that maimed them for life and cost their families' entire savings in medical expenses. The small metal ball that the children had mistakenly assumed was a harmless plaything? An unexploded submunition left over from cluster munitions used in warfare.

While this particular incident happened in Cambodia, there are hundreds of similar stories, from Laos, Vietnam, Kosovo, Serbia, Afghanistan, Iraq, Lebanon and many other countries, where children die or are injured while playing or walking to school, and men and women are killed in their backyards or working in their fields. When war is over, people get back to their homes, their schools and their communities, and try to pick up the pieces of their shattered lives. In conflicts where cluster munitions are used, in the aftermath of war, everyday activities are fraught with danger, as one wrong step can potentially kill or maim for a lifetime. The presence of unexploded remnants of war can halt development in countries for several years. Laos, one of the most bombed nations in the world, strewn with millions of submunitions, is still struggling to emerge from the devastating effects of the Vietnam War, more than four decades later.

Cluster bombs are weapons that are small but deadly. They often look like small metal canisters, and some of them are painted, giving them the innocuous appearance of a soda can. Each bomb contains within it hundreds or thousands of smaller submunitions, which disperse like the seeds of a dandelion over a wide area, also known as its footprint. Although the submunitions are meant to detonate on impact, various factors such as the height of dispersal, the ground quality and manufacturing defects, cause a large number (in some cases up to 30%) of the munitions to fail to detonate. In many cases, including one infamous example during the NATO campaign in Kosovo, the munitions miss their target entirely, instead landing on homes, hospitals and schools.

The unexploded submunitions that are scattered on the ground, in effect, act as landmines, that can kill or severely injure anyone who comes across them, sometimes even years and decades later. Given that military campaigns typically deploy thousands of these bombs at a time, each conflict leaves behind hundreds of thousands, sometimes millions, of these unpredictable mines, that make it hazardous for ordinary people to go about their daily lives once the conflict ends. A report by Handicap International reported that 98% of all casualties of cluster munitions are civilians, of which one-third are children. These injuries and fatalities occurred either because the munitions failed to land on the intended target, or from unexploded ordnance that failed to detonate on impact.

Despite all the problems associated with the use of these weapons, they are nevertheless an essential part of the military toolkit for many nations. Cluster munitions have been used in numerous conflicts in the past half-century, by at least 23 governments in 39 countries and four disputed territories since the Second World War. The users and producers of the weapons are major military powers, powers that have continued to use these weapons notwithstanding their substantial humanitarian costs. It has been estimated by the Cluster Munition Monitor that prior to 2006, 91 countries stockpiled cluster munitions containing a billion submunitions in their arsenals.

Given the inaccuracy of the weapons, the harm they cause even to the militaries that use them (for instance, in Afghanistan, the use of cluster munitions became so hazardous for the United States' troops that soldiers started to complain, because it slowed down their progress and caused deaths of Coalition soldiers) and the devastation that is left behind at the end of war, the continued use of these lethal weapons seemed outmoded. For decades, humanitarian organizations sought to limit the use of these weapons, but international consensus on the issue was hard to come by. As a UNDP representative stated: "The issue was too political, the problem too complicated, the process too stalled – in short, the obstacles to a Convention were simply too formidable to overcome".

In the fall of 2008, I was studying for a Masters' in Public Policy at Cornell University, in Ithaca, New York. I was taking a class at the law school on international cooperation, and having just completed six months as an intern at Human Rights Watch, I decided to write about the Oslo Process and the campaign to ban cluster munitions for my final paper, coincidentally presenting my work the day before the historic signing of the treaty at Oslo on December 3, 2008. The following year, I chose to expand this initial paper for my Master's thesis. My thesis attempted to explore the reasons behind the success of this accomplishment from the perspective of international relations. This book is based on that work, although it has been completely re-written (for the second time, for this revised and expanded edition), with additional research supplementing each section, as well as updated content to include the progress made since the adoption of the Convention.

Hence, in one way or another, I have been researching the topic of cluster munitions for over eight years, and still find myself endlessly fascinated by it. What keeps drawing me to this subject, and why I find this topic awe-inspiring is that at its very core, the story of how cluster munitions were banned is a story of the triumph of the underdog, the fight between David and Goliath. On one hand, a deadly but essential weapon used for the past half-century by the most powerful militaries in the world was pitted against a ragtag motley group of experienced as well as inexpert NGOs and victims' groups teamed up with a handful of committed-to-the-cause states, alongside behind-the-scenes support from advisory international organizations. In spite of the wealth of experience, knowledge and expertise possessed by the Cluster Munition Coalition (the group of NGOs and organizations working towards the cluster munition ban) and the United Nations as well as the International Committee of the Red Cross, they faced a monumental and nearly impossible task – to convince governments to agree to stop using a valuable weapon in their arsenals that they stockpiled by the hundreds of thousands, in a political climate where the interests of national security and state sovereignty outweighed humanitarian concerns in almost every instance.

Where many international agreements failed and diplomatic processes stalled, the campaign to ban cluster munitions succeeded. Despite strong opposition from many countries, including key military powers and Security Council members, 107 countries met in Dublin in May 2008 to negotiate and adopt a treaty prohibiting the use, production, transfer and stockpiling of cluster munitions. As of this writing, the Convention on Cluster Munitions has since been adopted by a total of 119 countries. The outcome of the Oslo Process was a ray of hope among the usual cynicism and disenchantment of similar international processes. As the United Kingdom's Secretary Of State For Foreign And Commonwealth Affairs, the Hon. David Miliband stated: "In less than two years…over one hundred countries have come together to conceive, plan, negotiate, agree, and now sign the most significant disarmament treaty of recent years".

The treaty was coincidentally signed on the 11th anniversary of the Mine Ban Treaty, another landmark moment in international history that marked the first instance of a successful partnership between states and civil society in achieving a staggering humanitarian objective. However, unlike in the case of landmines, the harm from the use of cluster munitions was not as well-established, and the cause did not benefit from celebrity endorsement. The success of this process goes against conventional theories about international relations, garnering questions about how this process was completed in record time, overcoming the strong objections of powerful international players and maintaining a tough treaty text. This book explores this question: how was this accomplished, and are there any wider lessons to be learned from it?

This book is written primarily chronologically, to make it easier to follow the journey from the early instances of cluster munition use to the ban and subsequent progress, while also tying in larger thematic elements along the way. Chapter 2 describes the nature of cluster munitions and their humanitarian effects, and gives an overview of the history of their use globally till the events leading up to the ban. Chapter 3 focuses on international law as it relates to cluster munitions, first providing a quick primer on the laws of war, then detailing the history of attempts to regulate cluster munitions within the larger context of weapons that affect civilians and cause unnecessary suffering. Chapter 4 describes the diplomatic process that eventually led to the treaty on cluster munitions. Chapter 5 highlights some of the obstacles and the key objections raised throughout the process. In chapter 6, I explain what I think are the primary factors that contributed to the discourse regarding cluster munition use changing seemingly rapidly from potential regulation to an outright ban that was supported by several current users and producers of the weapons. Chapter 7 describes the core provisions of the final agreement and analyses its main achievements and critiques. Chapter 8 lays out the progress made in implementing the provisions of the treaty so far, while contributing to the spread of a global norm against the use of cluster munitions, which will make it politically difficult even for non-signatory countries (those who haven't adopted the Convention) to use these weapons. Finally, chapter 9 concludes with some broader lessons from the process that can be applied to other humanitarian issues that require global solutions.

While this book will surely benefit students of international law, political science and diplomacy, as well as those working in NGOs or campaigns wishing to draw lessons from the success of the cluster munition ban campaign, I wrote this book for anyone with an interest in international politics and global affairs. I wrote this book because I was inspired by the example of a successful humanitarian outcome in an arena that is usually peppered instead with instances of compromise and concession. I believe that this story will inspire hope that the intractable problems that face our generation can be overcome with unity, determination and the willingness to believe in change. Steve Goose, co-chairman of the Cluster Munition Coalition stated at the Signing Conference in Oslo:

> We should celebrate…this extraordinary achievement. It is all the more extraordinary because of the ardent assertions we have endured about the so-called military necessity of cluster munitions. It is all the more extraordinary because of the international environment we have faced in which some believe that anything and everything can be done in the name of a global war on terror. We should celebrate both the convention itself and the manner in which it has been brought about: stepping outside the boundaries of traditional diplomacy, or at least stretching those boundaries considerably…

To celebrate the Convention is to understand the process behind it and distill its lessons so that we may replicate this remarkable achievement.

LETHAL LEGACY
THE NEED FOR A BAN

The time has come to agree that these weapons that cause such indiscriminate suffering should no longer be used. The time has come to agree that we need a new international instrument to ban cluster munitions that have unacceptable humanitarian consequences.
– Jonas Gahr Støre, Minister of Foreign Affairs (Norway), Oslo Conference

THE NEED FOR A BAN ON CLUSTER MUNITIONS WAS APPARENT FOR decades. Cluster munitions have been used with increasing frequency in armed conflict since the 1970s, and in each instance, they left devastation and destruction in their wake. This chapter explores the nature of cluster munitions, a brief overview of their history of use and the immediate and long-term effects of using these weapons.

The Nature of Cluster Munitions
Firstly, what exactly are cluster munitions? Cluster munitions

or cluster bombs are weapons that contain hundreds of smaller submunitions inside them, which burst when released. The Convention on Cluster Munitions defines a *cluster munition* as "a conventional munition that is designed to disperse or release explosive submunitions each weighing less than 20 kilograms..." They are analogous to dandelions, which have hundreds of spores that scatter over a wide area. Each 'spore' of a dandelion corresponds to the *submunitions* or *bomblets* within each munition, each of which is an individual weapon.

The weapon itself consists of a canister and several submunitions within it. Once dropped, the canister opens in mid-air and the submunitions scatter over the target, exploding on impact. These munitions can be launched from the air (releasing 'bomblets') or from the ground (releasing 'grenades').

The nature of cluster munitions and their effects have changed with changing technology. Initial forms of cluster bombs were created to primarily kill soldiers in battle, but the modern models are more complex. They contain scored shells which are intended to wound or kill by fragmenting, and anti-armor munitions that are designed to damage vehicles and defense materiel. These weapons are valued by militaries because they can easily cover a wide area and have multiple effects. Some models, such as the ones used in Afghanistan in 1999, had three ways of causing damage. The steel core, which broke into 300 jagged cores of metal, could injure people 500 feet away, and damage light armor and trucks 50 feet away. A concave cone at the bottom of the munition acted as an anti-armor weapon, piercing into tanks and similar vehicles. Finally, a zirconium wafer spread incendiary fragments that could burn nearby vehicles. These particular weapons are called *combined effects munitions* due to their multiple effects.

Cluster munitions, in general, are primarily used as area weapons, to destroy 'soft' targets such as airfields, by dispersing bomblets over the area. Their effects are not confined to one precise target, such as an individual tank for example, and can cover a large area. The area covered by the cluster munition once it is launched is called its *footprint*, and many types of cluster bombs have very wide footprints.

There are over 200 models of cluster munitions. Different models have different dispersal rates, depending on whether they adjust for the wind or not, and different *dud rates* (the percentage of submunitions in a cluster bomb that fails to explode when the bomb is launched), with older models having much higher dud rates. Depending on the dud rate and the dispersal area (or footprint), hundreds of thousands of *duds* (unexploded submunitions or ordnance) can litter over wide areas, remaining on the ground for decades after the end of the conflict, acting as a de-factor landmine for anyone who happens upon them.

History of Use

We must bring an end to the unacceptable human suffering caused by the use of cluster munitions. This suffering is not an inevitable and unavoidable consequence of modern war. It is the result of the use of a particular group of weapons, developed for other conflict scenarios than those we are faced with today.
- Jonas Gahr Støre, Minister of Foreign Affairs (Norway), Oslo Conference

Cluster munitions came to gain importance in warfare due to "a combination of technological innovations, changing combat needs, industrial interests, permissive laws, and lack of public awareness or debate". The initial concept of a 'cluster' or group of munitions first surfaced during the First World War, but came into more conventional use after World War II.

Further technological innovations during the Korean War made these munitions more effective, less expensive and a bigger part of the arsenal of major militaries such as the United States. In the aftermath of the Vietnam War, the US left millions of unexploded ordnance behind in Southeast Asia, that continued to injure and kill civilians in the intervening decades. Nonetheless, the US not only continued to use these weapons, they became an even bigger part of their armory, comprising nearly 29% of the United States Air Force's entire artillery budget. Use of cluster munitions in conflict in the 1970s and 1980s extended to Africa, the Americas, the Middle East, and South Asia.

The Soviet Union, another major user of cluster munitions, used them extensively during its invasion of Afghanistan from 1979 - 1989. The Russian government also used cluster munitions widely in Chechnya from 1994 - 1996, and again in 1999. In violation of the laws of war, Russia directed many of its cluster munition attacks, including the infamous 1999 attack on the Grozny market (which reportedly killed at least 137 people) at civilian areas.

Vietnam War

Cluster munitions are an especially heinous legacy of the Vietnam War. Technological advances and the unique challenges faced by the United States in Southeast Asia made the use of cluster munitions an integral part of their military strategy. The US dropped approximately 80,000 cluster munitions (containing 26 million submunitions) on Cambodia, more than 296,000 cluster munitions (containing nearly 97 million submunitions) on Vietnam, and more than 414,000 cluster munitions (containing at least 260 million submunitions) on Laos. The millions of unexploded ordnances left behind hindered the development of these countries for decades, affecting an already impoverished populace. Cluster munitions fueled opposition to the Vietnam War both inside and outside the US, as protestors highlighted the destructive effects of these munitions in their campaigns, and journalists reported on the damage wrought by them.

Between 1964 and 1973, the United States dropped cluster bombs on Laos during the Vietnam War every eight minutes, leaving behind between 20 - 60 million unexploded submunitions. The planes used to bomb Laos were fitted to carry about 30 tons of bombs, many of them failing to detonate, with a failure rate as high as 30%. Estimates by the United Nations put at least 500,000 unexploded ordnance (UXO) still in the country in 1996. Due to the high number of duds left behind after the war, between 1973 and 2006, over 4,800 casualties have been reported in Lao, although according to the International Committee of the Red Cross (ICRC), the figure is closer to 11,000, more than 30% of whom were children. Accidents and injuries related to the unexploded ordnances are common, with 65% of those injuries occurring while performing everyday tasks such as working in the fields.

Cluster munitions were used in Cambodia from 1969 - 73, to stop supplies and troops traveling along the Ho Chi Minh Trail. Strikes during that period are said to have left behind an estimated 1.9 - 5.7 million submunitions. Although the failure rate of the munitions was projected by the United States at 10%, it has been estimated by Handicap International that the actual failure rate was closer to 30% due to various factors on the ground, including the method of deployment of the munitions. This would imply that between 0.5 – 1.7 million submunitions failed to detonate, and was left behind as de-facto landmines, to injure or kill hundreds and thousands of people in the aftermath of the conflict.

In Vietnam, the number of submunitions left behind is reported at between 7 - 20 million, leading to 1,275 reported casualties. The reported numbers are a fraction of estimated casualty figures, based on various data points collected by Handicap International. They estimate the actual casualty figures in Vietnam between 1975 and 2006 to be closer to 34,500 - 52,350. The other casualty figures cited previously in Laos and Cambodia are also estimated to be inaccurate by several thousand.

First Gulf War

The United States used cluster munitions extensively during the first Gulf War; cluster bombs accounted for a quarter of the bombs dropped on Iraq and Kuwait. Cluster bombs were used against a range of targets, including infrastructure and dual-use targets also used by civilians. To avoid anti-aircraft fire, the bombs were dropped from medium to high altitudes, a factor that increased the number of duds. Additional factors such as the desert soil and the high number of munitions used in total raised the dud rates, and contributed to high civilian casualties. Unexploded ordnances also killed or injured one hundred US soldiers, and killed a hundred clearance workers.

Yugoslavia and Kosovo

Cluster munitions were used by NATO, Serbian forces and other internal factions in the Kosovo conflict in 1999, along the Albania - Kosovo border, in Bosnia and Herzegovina, and in Croatia. Although there were fewer cluster bombs dropped in (the former) Yugoslavia than in previous conflicts (cluster bombs accounted for 7% of all bombs), they accounted for a larger number of civilian deaths. Around 150 civilians died during cluster bomb strikes, and following a much-publicized incident where a bomb mistakenly targeted a civilian area due to technical failure, US President Bill Clinton temporarily suspended the use of cluster bombs in the campaign. In Kosovo, cluster munitions used by NATO caused at least 164 recorded casualties, mainly of children. Deaths from cluster bomb ordnance in the aftermath of the war represent 10% of all civilian deaths throughout the war.

Afghanistan

Cluster bombs were an important part of the United States' military arsenal in their war against terror in Afghanistan, with the US dropping over 1,200 bombs containing more than 248,000 bomblets between October 2001 and March 2002. Human Rights Watch reports that at least 25 civilians were killed immediately from cluster bomb attacks, although the actual figures could be substantially greater, as there are usually large discrepancies between reported and real casualty data. Even after the end of combat, unexploded bomblets or 'duds' left behind continue to cause fatalities. Despite using conservative estimates of failure rates, there are reported to be over 10,000 unexploded bomblets strewn over villages and fields in Afghanistan.

The United States used cluster bombs in Afghanistan on four major types of targets - frontlines, military bases, cave complexes and villages where Taliban or Al-Qaeda forces were hiding. While the targeting of frontlines or military bases with cluster bombs was legitimate under international law at the time, targeting villages with non-combatants is never considered legitimate under international humanitarian law. Most of the civilian casualties from cluster bomb strikes took place in villages that were targeted as part of the operation. The Taliban soldiers also intentionally hid in villages, using the villagers as 'human shields' to save themselves, violating the *principle of distinction* in international humanitarian law, which requires the separation of combatants and civilians during conflict.

In the aftermath of the war, at least 127 fatalities, mostly children, were reported as a result of cluster munition duds or unexploded ordnances. The most common instances of civilian death resulted from undertaking everyday activities such as gathering wood and herding sheep. Gathering the scrap metal from the casings of bombs to sell at the market also caused many of the duds strewn around the casings to be set off, an, unfortunately, common occurrence among an impoverished populace that felt compelled to seize the opportunity of additional income from scrap gathering.

The bombs dropped in Afghanistan were dangerous in another way - the yellow color of the canisters resembled the yellow food aid parcels dropped for those in the midst of the war zone. Human Rights Watch stated that "[i]t is highly likely that many in Afghanistan will *not know* the difference between aerially delivered food aid and aerially delivered munitions" (emphasis added). Amidst ensuing outcry over the danger of the villagers mistaking the bombs for the food aid parcels, the United States changed the color of the aid packages.

Iraq War

In the 2003 war against Iraq, in three weeks of hostilities, the Coalition forces used 13,000 cluster munitions. Many of the air attacks which resulted in the deaths of scores of civilians occurred while targeting senior Iraqi officials. These attacks were based on imprecise intelligence, and all of them failed to kill any of the intended targets, instead causing many civilian casualties. During and after the war, unexploded ordnances caused hundreds of civilian deaths, impeded Coalition troop movements and caused the deaths of Coalition soldiers. The humanitarian and military impact arising from these weapons even caused some of the US soldiers fighting in Iraq to themselves call for an end to using these weapons.

Due to the number of munitions used, a dud rate of even 5% would leave around 90,000 duds or unexploded ordnance. Thousands of these duds were left behind in villages and towns where

Iraqi forces had occupied areas near civilian populations. The Coalition forces also used large quantities of Vietnam-era cluster munitions that had far higher failure rates, some of them nearing 30%.

Lebanon

During Israel's 34-day war with Lebanon in July and August 2006, it used over four million submunitions on South Lebanon, a large majority of which was in the final days of the war. According to the UNDP, as of February 2007, 841 individual locations of new cluster bomb strikes were confirmed spread over an area of more than 34 million square meters. It is estimated by clearance experts that the munitions averaged a failure rate of 25%, indicating that up to one million submunitions were spread over homes, fields and neighborhoods in more than 40 towns and villages in Lebanon. Tragically, this attack came on the heels of concerted clearance efforts by UN Mine Action Service and other organizations, that had cleared over 2 million square meters of land previously affected by cluster munition strikes in Southern Lebanon.

Globally, the attacks by Israel against Lebanon were the most extensive use of cluster munitions since the 1991 Gulf War - more than twice the number used in Iraq in 2003, and 15 times more than that used in Afghanistan in 2001 - 2002. Both civilian and de-miner casualties have been considerable since the end of the hostilities, and agriculture has been severely disrupted due to the presence of thousands of submunitions in the fields.

Since the Convention on Cluster Munitions was negotiated, there have been several instances of use of cluster munitions (documented in chapter 7), although no use has been reported by states that adopted the cluster munition ban.

Humanitarian Effects of Cluster Munition Use

[T]he presence of unexploded sub-munitions bomblets cause not only a physical harm and death to the civilians but also constitute a long-term obstacle to the socio-economic reconstruction of the affected countries.
- Dr. Thongloun Sisoulith, Deputy Prime Minister (Lao PDR), Oslo Signing Ceremony

The widespread use of cluster munitions in conflicts around the world have created a wide range of humanitarian problems, contributing significantly to security concerns in the immediate aftermath of conflict, as well as hampering development and rehabilitation of the affected areas years, sometimes decades, after the cessation of hostilities.

Cluster munitions cause two main humanitarian problems: firstly, because they disperse widely, the weapon cannot distinguish between civilian and military targets, which can have devastating consequences in populated areas; and secondly, those that fail to explode act like anti-personnel mines, killing and maiming those who encounter them, sometimes years after a conflict has ended. Thus, the use of these weapons has two primary effects: i) immediate effects and ii) after-effects.

Immediate Effects

Cluster submunitions (the individual munitions within the larger canister) are designed to kill, unlike its close cousin, landmines, which were originally designed to maim, rather than cause death. Due to the way these weapons are designed, they cause more fatalities than landmines. The effects of cluster munitions are thus even more dangerous if the submunitions or duds litter an area frequented by civilians or the dud rate (the number of submunitions that fail to go off at the point of impact) is high due to various factors such as poor design or use of the weapon in inappropriate environments. Civilians are the most vulnerable after a cluster munition attack, as it has been estimated that 98% of fatalities caused by cluster munitions are civilians; in other words, only 2% of the time, cluster munitions are successful at hitting their intended target. A Human Rights Watch report on the impact of cluster munitions found that "children are particularly common victims. The shape and sometimes color of submunitions attracts them because they are curious and believe the weapons are toys. Some models resemble balls while others have a ribbon, which makes a convenient handle for carrying or twirling".

Most cluster bombs are 'dumb bombs', because they are unguided and imprecise. Once the weapon is dropped, it opens, and the hundreds of 'bomblets' disperse over a wide area. Factors such as the level of wind and the height from which it has been dropped affect the footprint of the bomb (the area covered by the bomblets); thus, often inadvertently targeting civilian populations near the area. Even if the bomb hits its intended target precisely, civilians in or near the footprint can be affected. "In every conflict involving cluster munition use that Human Rights Watch has investigated, the weapons have been used in areas where both combatants and civilians are present, resulting in loss of civilian life." Where civilian and military personnel live in close proximity, or when the bombs are dropped in places also inhabited by civilians, the civilian casualty rates can be even higher.

The United States, in its defense of the use of cluster bombs, has suggested that cluster bombs cause less destruction than unitary bomb strikes, using the example that in Afghanistan, cluster bombs left holes in walls of civilian homes, but did not completely destroy their structures like other bombs do. Unfortunately, this reasoning is specious, because it does not take into account the fact that targeting civilians at all is absolutely prohibited by the Geneva Conventions that govern the rules of warfare, whether by cluster bombs or any other kind of bomb. Additionally, due to the nature of cluster bombs (their tendency to drift off target, and the nature of their dispersal on the ground), it is not always possible to prevent accidentally targeting civilian areas, thus causing those nations that employ them to be particularly likely to violate the laws of war.

Handicap International (HI), co-winner of the Nobel Peace Prize for its work on banning landmines, has compiled evidence of at least 13,306 confirmed casualties from the use of cluster munitions during conflict, which is an accurate tally of figures worldwide as of 2007. This number only includes *confirmed* figures, the estimated casualty figures are between 55,000 and 100,000. The data on casualties from cluster munitions is not easy to find, and in some cases, it simply does not exist. Only 12% of cluster munitions affected countries have nearly complete records about cluster munitions, 64% have limited data, while 20% of countries affected have no data at all. Both military and civilian casualties were underreported in most countries. The figures do confirm, however, that almost 98% of all cluster munitions casualties are civilians. This is predominantly because most cluster munitions strikes occurred on or near civilian populated areas, dual-use areas, and sometimes even exclusively civilian targets.

Technological innovations in certain instances also served to make the weapons even more lethal, as experiments determined that small, high-velocity projectiles were most effective at causing injury. The weapons were designed to fragment to the greatest possible extent, as well as disperse widely, to cause damage to the largest possible area. This, and the addition of time-release fuses ensured that the cluster bombs would be able to kill the highest number of targets possible, over time. Unfortunately, the weapons are unable to distinguish between intended and unintended targets, and their lethal capacities lead to the deaths of large numbers of unintended targets, an uncontrollable factor once the weapons have already been deployed.

A further, more chilling aspect of the use of cluster munitions, is that they are sold by producers of cluster munitions to armed non-state groups, and it is possible that they could use the weapons to disrupt humanitarian relief efforts and perhaps deliberately use the weapons against civilians to create terror. This is not a completely far-off scenario, as it has been alleged that much of Hezbollah's use of cluster munitions against Israeli citizens in the 2006 war was part of a campaign to deliberately target enemy civilians. There is also a danger that as newer technology for cluster munitions emerges, the older stockpiles will be transferred by countries to allies with less advanced military armory.

After Effects

In post-conflict settings around the world, explosive remnants of cluster munitions undermine hard won development gains. As surely as poverty, gender inequality and the absence of basic social services, cluster munitions make the achievement of the Millennium Development Goals impossible.
– Kathleen Cravero, UNDP, Oslo Signing Conference

The after effects of cluster bomb use are even more deleterious, and one of the main drivers of the campaign to ban these weapons. Many of the hundreds of bomblets that comprise each weapon fail to detonate upon impact, leaving behind 'dud' bomblets as unexploded ordnances. These ordnances act as "de-facto landmines", creating a hazard for civilians returning to the scene afterward. The bomblets are especially volatile and have been responsible for thousands of civilian deaths months and years after the end of hostilities. Years, sometimes even decades later, cluster submunitions continue to kill civilians in disproportionately high numbers. In some areas of Iraq for instance, up to 80% of all civilian casualties during the war resulted from cluster munition duds. In Afghanistan, between October 2001 and June 2002, dud bomblets from cluster bombs killed four times as many civilians as any other types of ordnance. There are several ways in which cluster submunitions can impact the area in which they were used long after the end of the conflict.

Agriculture and Rural Communities

The presence of unexploded ordnance severely impacts agricultural development, as farmers are often killed while tilling their land, hitting the duds with their plows. A United Nations Institute for Disarmament Research (UNIDIR) report in 2006 found that cluster munitions are particularly dangerous because of their long-lasting humanitarian impact and their effect on socio-economic development in rural areas. As Kathleen Cravero from UNDP stated: "If communities cannot work their lands, ply their trades or tend their cattle, they cannot and will not move forward". Handicap International reported in 2006 that 25% of villages in Laos were still affected by unexploded ordnance from cluster bombs dropped during the Vietnam War. As the duds are often scattered over arable land, they affect the agriculture of the region and cause villagers to lose their livelihood. Mr. Peter Batchelor, the representative from UNDP at the Oslo Conference, described the wider impact of these weapons on development: "Beyond their humanitarian impact, cluster munitions can also directly and indirectly impede states' abilities to achieve the Millennium Development Goals. Put another way, those countries that are affected by cluster munitions will struggle to achieve the MDGs."

Aside from the loss of livelihood, the trauma to the victim and their family caused by loss of life and limb can further create problems in the social fabric of the community, and can often require psycho-social counseling. As Mr. Batchelor affirmed, "survivors of cluster munitions accidents often face lifelong disabilities and economic constraints to access adequate physical and socio-economic assistance". Many families end up spending their entire life savings on medical costs and have to additionally deal with the psychological trauma for decades after the accident.

Refugees and IDPs

The presence of cluster bombs also hampers the return of refugees and internally displaced persons (IDPs) to the area. The number of casualties attributed to cluster submunitions reaches a peak just after the end of hostilities, when refugees return to their homes and communities. Women and children are particularly affected. The bombs rendering their villages and towns unsafe, Afghanistan's pre-existing refugee problem became more acute after the 2001 war, as United Nations' repatriation efforts slowed down till the villages could be deemed safe. Many refugees returned to potentially unsafe environments despite the risks, which were yet to be cleared of the submunitions. In Lao PDR and Lebanon, young males at work were disproportionately affected post-conflict. 84% of casualties of cluster submunitions have been found to be male, usually occurring while farming, tending animals, or in the case of young children, playing. Since the men in these countries are traditionally the main source of income, the communities are particularly hard-hit, and further disadvantaged economically.

.   .   .

Military Operations

The harmful effects of cluster munitions aren't limited to civilians. The use of cluster bombs causes problems for military operations that take place after their use. In Afghanistan, for instance, in areas where cluster bombs had been used, the presence of duds hampered the movement of the US troops, preventing movement at night. This severely eroded their advantage over the enemy, since the United States possessed night vision technology which allowed them to advance at night.

Immediate and comprehensive clearance of submunitions can put a stop to continuing post-strike civilian casualties. Although cluster bomb clearance is essential to prevent casualties, it is often delayed due to cost and political considerations. Dud clearance requires special training, equipment, and most of all, funds, which usually the countries affected by the munitions are unable to adequately resource.

Using Technology To Minimize Impact

Technical improvements in weapons technology will not be enough to address the complex humanitarian problems caused by cluster munitions.
- Jonas Gahr Støre, Minister of Foreign Affairs (Norway), Oslo Conference

It has been suggested that the best way to deal with the effects of cluster munitions is to simply regulate them, by ensuring that only those with a certain failure rate are employed, or that they are not used under certain battle conditions, such as near civilians. The United States has argued that the solution to the problem of cluster munition duds would be to work on improving the existing technology, and mandate that only those munitions that have a 99% reliability rate should be allowed to be deployed. However, even the 99% reliability rate would mean that thousands, sometimes hundreds of thousands, of submunitions would still fail, due to the large numbers of weapons that are deployed at one time.

At the same time, the arms control approach "assumes that all actors in fact abide by the rules regulating the use of weapons", which has been shown not to be the case. It isn't always possible to anticipate battle conditions in advance, and there are many factors that dictate the dud rate of cluster bombs used during a particular conflict. The rate of failure of the bombs is primarily determined by their model and design, which are influenced significantly by cost considerations. Several other factors can also increase the failure rate, such as the softness of the soil where the munitions are deployed, the collision of canisters in the air (which crush the canisters and can damage them) and dropping them from higher altitudes than are mandated. Thus, the dud rate of a weapon may be lower during laboratory testing, but the way it is deployed in the field could double or triple the number of unexploded ordnance that gets left behind.

Technology innovations have tried to focus on the problem of reducing dud rates, through the introduction of self-destruct and self-deactivation mechanisms. This addition did not lead to lower casualty rates, for two reasons. Firstly, troops were negligent in properly targeting the munitions, failing to avoid hitting civilian targets, assuming that the self-destruct mechanisms would compensate for their neglect and negate the danger to civilian life. Secondly, the self-destruct mechanisms were not as accurate as portrayed, as the mine clearance experts found in the aftermath of Israel's attack on Lebanon in 2006, where the models fitted with self-destructs were used widely, without significantly reducing the extent of unexploded ordnance.

Some newer models of cluster bombs have been adjusted for better targeting capacity, by adding in a Wind Corrected Munitions Dispenser (WCMD) to compensate for the effects of wind and to improve targeting accuracy. Evidence gathered by NGOs and clearance workers suggest that the WCMD did not compensate sufficiently, and thus has not significantly lowered civilian casualties. More advanced models have also introduced features such as infrared and laser sensor guidance systems, which are designed to seek out targets that have a high heat-signature, such as tanks and grounded aircraft, and failing to find such targets, to deactivate. However, there is currently insufficient evidence as to the veracity of these claims, and to what extent they perform as claimed.

Additionally, these weapons are more expensive, and have been used along with, rather than instead of, the older models. For instance, in the US' wars in Afghanistan and Iraq in 2001 and 2003 respectively, munitions dating from the time of the Vietnam era were used, which are known to have record-high dud rates. It is also likely, that older models of cluster munitions, as in the past, would be sold off to technologically less-developed countries, causing simply the location of the threat to civilian life to be changed, not the extent of the threat itself. For instance, in the 2006 war against Lebanon, Israel used munitions manufactured by the US in 1973, which resulted in abnormally high failure rates and considerable amounts of unexploded ordnance.

Thus, while the technological advancements were advertised as causing cluster munitions to be safer and more humane, in reality, they only created the perception of the use of cluster munitions being less dangerous, which caused them to be in effect even riskier. This is the same logic that people sometimes use when driving more recklessly while wearing a seat belt - the wearing of the seatbelt does not necessarily negate the effects of an accident, it only potentially reduces them. And wearing a seat-belt cannot be an excuse to ignore the rules of the road; just as, technological improvements in weaponry cannot be an excuse to ignore the rules of war (the laws governing the conduct of armed conflict).

Given the widespread use of cluster munitions, often hundreds of thousands of bombs carrying millions of submunitions at a time, and their combined short and longer term devastating effects, human rights organizations and those involved with clearance and the aftermath of their use in conflict sought to, regulate and severely limit at the very least, and ideally ban, their use for decades. Unfortunately, for many years, the rhetoric that the weapons were necessary for military purposes, and that their use wasn't any more detrimental than the use of other munitions, prevented any significant progress towards their regulation or restriction in international law. The next chapter details the progression in international fora of attempts to regulate and minimize the impact of anti-personnel mines and explosive remnants in the aftermath of war.

2

FAILURES IN DIPLOMACY

INTERNATIONAL HUMANITARIAN LAW AND EXPLOSIVE REMNANTS OF WAR

There is a growing recognition that the use of such cluster munitions often gives rise to violations of core provisions of the Geneva Conventions.

– Jonas Gahr Støre, Minister of Foreign Affairs (Norway), Oslo Conference

INTERNATIONAL LAW IS THE UMBRELLA TERM FOR ALL THE RULES and laws that govern the interactions between states, including laws for trade, laws governing the oceans and laws that set out the rules for conflict and warfare. The previous chapter described the main reasons why activists and victims believed that the problems with the use of cluster munitions were so pervasive as to need an outright ban on their use. The problems associated with cluster munitions can be broadly said to stem from their primary characteristic of leaving unexploded submunitions on the battlefield (which might include residential and urban areas) which cause problems in the immediate aftermath or at a later time. A ban or limitation on the global use of a weapon requires determining whether the interpretation of existing law might cover the limitation, or enacting a new law to govern its use.

This chapter gives an overview of the existing international law that relates to the use of weapons on the battlefield, with a specific focus on laws that would affect the use of cluster munitions. It also describes the history of efforts to regulate the broader area of explosive remnants of war and the steps that were taken to limit and control the impact of unexploded ordnance in warfare in the years preceding the Oslo Process.

The Laws of War

International humanitarian law (IHL), also called the law of war or the law of armed conflict, is the branch of international law that governs the rules of warfare, and describes what conduct is prohibited during armed conflict. According to the International Committee of the Red Cross (ICRC), international humanitarian law "is a set of rules which seek, for humanitarian reasons, *to limit the effects of armed conflict*". It primarily covers the protection of those who are not combatants (i.e. they are not fighting or have stopped fighting), as well as provides restrictions on the means, especially the types of weapons, that may be used, and methods, or their usage and tactics, of warfare. Therefore, in order to ban or stop the usage of a particular weapon, either its use has to be considered illegal under the existing laws of war, or a new law must be enacted to ban its usage.

An Overview of International Humanitarian Law

The primary tenets of international humanitarian law are prescribed in the four Geneva Conventions of 1949, as well as the two Additional Protocols of 1977. Almost all countries in the world have ratified (agreed to be bound by) the Geneva Conventions, and they are also considered to be part of customary international law, or law that all applies to all states.

One of the primary guiding principles of international humanitarian law is that it requires parties to a conflict to distinguish between combatants and non-combatants or civilians during warfare. The rules governing armed combat between states (or in some cases states and non-state armed groups) exist to protect both combatants and civilians, and its principles therefore limit the circumstances and means through which hostilities may take place between nations under international law. Article 48 of Additional Protocol I to the Geneva Convention states: "the Parties to the conflict shall at all times distinguish between the civilian population and combatants and between civilian objects and military objectives and accordingly shall direct their operations only against military objectives". The primary considerations of the rules of international humanitarian law are there to ensure that combatants maintain a sense of balance, and use weapons and methods of warfare that achieve their military objectives without descending into unnecessary brutality. Additional Protocol I therefore states that "it is prohibited to employ weapons, projectiles and material and methods of warfare of a nature *to cause superfluous injury or unnecessary suffering*" (emphasis added).

Weapons or methods of warfare that do not adhere to these rules are forbidden in international law. This objective is stated in Additional Protocol I to the Geneva Conventions: "In any armed conflict, the right of the Parties to the conflict to choose methods or means of warfare is not unlimited." Additional Protocol I further details the protection that is afforded to civilians or non-combatants under the Geneva Convention. Article 51 of the Additional Protocol states that civilians themselves cannot be under attack, and "acts or threats of violence the primary purpose of which is to spread terror among the civilian population are prohibited". The same article also prohibits indiscriminate attacks, those that are not targeted at a "specific military objective", those "which employ a method or means of combat which cannot be directed at a specific military objective" and those attacks employing means that "are of a nature to strike military objectives and civilians or civilian objects without distinction". Attacks that are deemed indiscriminate include those that treat several different military objectives in an area containing civilians and civilian objects as one military objective, and an attack that might cause civilian casualties which "would be excessive in relation to the concrete and direct military advantage anticipated". Thus, weapons and types of combat that are not able to discriminate between combatants and civilian targets are prohibited unequivocally under the laws of armed conflict.

Additional Protocol I also directs the type of precautions that are needed to be taken to protect civilians. The states involved must "take all feasible precautions in the choice of means and methods of attack with a view to avoiding, and in any event minimising, incidental loss" to the lives and property of civilians, and "refrain from deciding to launch any attack which may be expected to cause incidental loss" to civilians "which would be excessive in relation to the concrete and direct military advantage anticipated". In the context of international humanitarian law, "protection" means that certain categories of persons (those who are not fighting, such as civilians as well as medical and religious military personnel) are entitled to respect regarding their life and must be treated humanely, under all circumstances. There are specific rules that forbid killing or wounding soldiers who surrender or are unable to fight, and ones that mandate states to care for the wounded, as well as protect of medical personnel, ambulances and hospitals from attack.

Therefore, as stated by Norwegian Deputy Minister of Defence, Mr Espen Barth-Eide: "The use of cluster munitions, like the use of all other types of weapons, is restricted by the general obligations, on the one hand, to distinguish between military

objectives and civilians, between combatants and non-combatants, and, on the other hand, not to conduct attacks where the
civilian harm caused is disproportionate to the military gain
expected from the attack...States disagree, however, on how these
rules should be interpreted and implemented in practice with
regard to the use of cluster munitions." The use of cluster munitions is bound by the existing laws of war and conduct by states,
and it can be argued that their use violated the principles of
international humanitarian law even before the start of the Oslo
process.

How Use of Cluster Munitions Violate International Humanitarian Law

The use of cluster munitions arguably violates an important
principle of the law of armed conflict - the need to distinguish
between enemy combatants and civilians. As discussed in the
previous chapter, whether as a result of mistaken targeting, the
wide footprint of the weapon or due to the unexploded ordnance
they leave behind, cluster munitions cannot effectively distinguish
between soldiers and civilians, and consequently appear to violate
Article 48 of Additional Protocol I. As estimated by Handicap
International, 98% of the victims of cluster munition attacks are
civilians, indicating clearly that far from differentiating between
types of victims, cluster munitions primarily cause harm to non-
combatants who are ostensibly protected by international
humanitarian law. Cluster munitions, because they contain
hundreds of pieces of shrapnel designed to cause maximum
damage to personnel as well as military targets, can arguably be
said to "cause superfluous injury or unnecessary suffering", which
is also prohibited by Additional Protocol I of the Geneva
Convention.

Additionally, the provisions of Article 51 (on preventing civilians from being attacked and prohibiting indiscriminate attacks)

may be interpreted to prohibit most uses of cluster munitions, as they typically cannot be employed in such a way as to focus on a specific military target, without affecting the surrounding areas. While some states have not ratified Additional Protocol I (the United States for instance), these provisions are considered to be part of customary international law, and thus applicable to all states.

Another important principle of IHL is the *proportionality test*, which prohibits attacks when the expected civilian harm is greater than the anticipated benefit from the attack. This principle is articulated in Additional Protocol I as well as a being a part of customary international law. Under the proportionality test of Protocol I the military advantage of the attack must be balanced against its civilian impact. Strikes using cluster munitions arguably fail this proportionality test, as they impact an area far greater than the specific target of the attack and impact civilians disproportionately. An August 2001 U.S. Air Force background paper acknowledges that cluster munitions "must pass [the] proportionality test" and states that there are "clearly some areas where [cluster bombs] normally couldn't be used (e.g., populated city centers)". Some legal experts further argue that the proportionality test takes into account the aftereffects of cluster munition use, since the effects of unexploded ordnance from cluster munitions far exceeds that from other weapons.

Cluster munitions can be arguably indiscriminate weapons, as their footprint cannot always be controlled, and certain models and conditions of use can cause significant unexploded ordnance and possibly "excessive" damage, especially in relation to the level of military advantage that they provide in the majority of scenarios. In modern urban warfare, most notably in conflicts in Afghanistan, Iraq, Lebanon and most recently Georgia and Syria, precise targeting of military targets is almost impossible with these weapons, and the benefit attained is not proportional to the damage to civilians' life and livelihood. Invariably the weapons either miss their target, or as is often the case in urban warfare, civilians within the footprint of the munitions deployed are injured or killed. The aftereffects, especially in recent conflicts, can be so deleterious as to make the use of cluster bombs in such contexts completely disproportional in almost all cases. In South Lebanon for instance, Israel's blanketing over 850 strike sites with cluster munitions in the last three days before a settlement was imminent can be seen to be violating the *proportionality principle*.

As stated by the International Committee of the Red Cross, "... these issues raise serious questions as to whether such weapons can be used in populated areas in accordance with fundamental rules of international humanitarian law including the rule of proportionality and the prohibition of indiscriminate attacks". It can thus be argued that the use of cluster munitions can be seen as a breach of the pre-existing norms and principles of international law, particularly that of international humanitarian law as covered by the Geneva Convention of 1949 and its Additional Protocols. However, given that cluster munitions were widely used in many military conflicts, in order to change the norms regarding their usage, it would be unrealistic to expect most states to abide by an implicit and debatable violation, and therefore it was necessary for states to specifically agree to ban the use of the weapons, by creating new law codifying their intention.

A Brief History of Weapons Regulation

The idea that military force and the use of specific weapon types should be regulated by international conventions is not a novel idea. The first rules governing the use of force can be traced back to ancient civilizations and religions.
– Mr. Espen Barth-Eide, Norway Deputy Minister of Defense, Oslo Conference

While international humanitarian law provides general protection to civilians and non-combatants from unnecessary injury during armed conflict, there are no agreements that specifically deal with the harmful effects of cluster munitions. The general principles of international humanitarian law provide a cogent argument against the use of cluster munitions, but they are difficult to enforce. As the International Committee of the Red Cross stated, "although it could be argued that the general rules of international humanitarian law are sufficient, it is unlikely that they will be applied in an adequate or consistent manner unless specific rules for ERW (explosive remnants of war) are adopted. Clear rules will help identify the minimum norms expected of parties to a conflict and promote their implementation on a broad scale". Thus, in order to protect against the harmful effects of cluster munitions and unexploded ordnances, new international agreements regulating these weapons would be needed.

Early Attempts to Regulate Harmful Weapons: Committees and Conferences

As early as the 1950s, the International Committee of the Red Cross (ICRC) began to draft rules that would limit the types of weapons that states could use in combat, as a direct response to the ravages experienced as a result of military advancements in destructive technologies and the use of biological and chemical weapons during the Second World War. Although there was insufficient support to turn these rules into an international agreement, it served as a first step towards codifying humanitarian principles of warfare.

Concerns that a number of weapons used in the Indochina war were violating two principles of international humanitarian law: avoiding unnecessary suffering, and prohibiting indiscriminate attack, led to the commission of research and studies on the effects of various weapons. During the Vietnam War, Cambodia, Vietnam and Laos were devastated with the widespread use of cluster bombs and anti-personnel mines by the United States, many of the attacks occurring in civilian areas. In fact, one estimate concluded that between 1965 and 1973 the United States dropped at least 14.3 million tonnes of munitions in Indochina, almost double the amount employed throughout the Second World War. The human toll of the use of these munitions set back development in these countries by decades: in Lao for instance, considered the most heavily bombed nation in the world per capita, 15 of its 17 provinces were affected by the presence of unexploded ordnances, littering fields, roads, rivers and schoolyards. Although at the time the United States downplayed the impact of its use of cluster munitions, journalists and activists reporting on the war spread awareness of the devastation wrought by the use of weapons that clearly violated the tenets of protecting civilians and non-combatants from being targeted during armed conflict.

By 1971, the International Committee of the Red Cross (ICRC) had convened a Conference of Government Experts to study their draft rules regarding armed conflict, including restricting the use of weapons that caused "excessive injury" or had "indiscriminate effects". Following that conference, the Swiss government (in its capacity as the depositary for the Geneva Conventions) convened a body, the Diplomatic Conference on the Reaffirmation and Development of International Humanitarian Law (or the CDDH) to negotiate Additional Protocols to the Geneva Convention based on the ICRC drafts.

The rules that were being discussed were general and included a wide category of weapons. It was clear that the manifest problems associated with the use of many of the new military technologies and the inadequacy of current international law on this issue necessitated a comprehensive treaty dealing with this problem. At this time, the humanitarian impact associated specifically with the use of cluster munitions was increasingly apparent, and in 1974, states attending the Conference of Governmental Experts on Weapons that May Cause Unnecessary Suffering or Have Indiscriminate Effect (as part of and concurrently with the CDDH negotiations) called for a ban on cluster munitions (among other weapons such as incendiary weapons and anti-personnel mines), and reiterated the same in another conference in 1976 at Lugano. These calls for action coincided with the widespread use of cluster munitions in South-east Asia. However, lack of consensus among states tabled those discussions. As John Borrie stated in his book on the subject, "cluster munitions would remain off the multilateral negotiating table for the next 27 years". The divergence in views came from certain European and developing states on the one hand, who were in favor of limiting the high-technology, most inhumane weapons, and the major military powers on the other hand, who objected either to restrictions on any scale or to the venue of the negotiations. As UNIDIR Director Patricia Lewis argued at the Oslo Conference, states opposed to regulations "...use a number of techniques to block progress both in the structures in which they operate and by proxy through complementary structures and small cooperative groups". This rift and these objections were repeated during the Oslo Process.

The Convention on Certain Conventional Weapons

The negotiations and conferences made clear that specific weapons would be difficult to ban, but a general consensus emerged agreeing to negotiate these issues within the United Nations framework. This consensus led to the adoption in 1980 of the Convention on Certain Conventional Weapons (also known as the CCW), which served as an "umbrella" convention. The CCW consisted of a general agreement and a number of protocols on specific weapons, which would allow the possibility of adding new protocols in the future, leaving room for states to negotiate further agreements as weapons technology became more advanced. Additional protocols were adopted in 1995 and 2003, that expanded the ambit of the convention to include other weapons.

According to the International Committee of the Red Cross, the purpose of the CCW was to apply two general customary rules of international humanitarian law to specific weapons: 1) the prohibition on using weapons that are indiscriminate (that do not distinguish between combatants and non-combatants) and 2) the prohibition on the use of weapons that cause unnecessary suffering or superfluous injury. The CCW applies not only to international armed conflicts, but to all conflicts (it was amended in 1996 to include non-international armed conflicts as well).

The adoption of the CCW resulted from a compromise which allowed broader support for the agreement in exchange for a less rigorous outcome. Those who would have preferred a more robust mechanism, felt that "military considerations had been given much greater priority than humanitarian concerns". The three initial protocols that were negotiated at the same time as the umbrella agreement further failed to break much ground, with only Protocol I banning a type of weapon. Protocol II established regulations on the use, transfer and clearance of antipersonnel landmines and Protocol III prohibited the use of air-delivered incendiary devices against civilians. In the first few years of the CCW's existence, the treaty was deemed unimportant and forgotten; however, after the 1995 review conference, the number of adoptions to the CCW increased, and the intense debate around the issue of landmines gave more prominence to the convention. It was at this point that the focus shifted to consider the related issue of explosive remnants of war (ERW).

Despite earlier calls to ban cluster munitions, they had not been dealt with as a specific weapons category at the international level and was only alluded to in the 1980 Convention on Certain

Conventional Weapons. International action resulted in the ban of anti-personnel mines in 1997, but a treaty on cluster munitions was shelved for the time being. As UNIDIR Director Lewis stated, "on the whole, disarmament efforts have lagged behind technological advances and have been responses to the humanitarian consequences of weapons, rather than foresighted safeguards. Moreover, it's been especially tough to deal with the choice of weapons when those weapons are perceived as militarily useful."

Cluster munitions continued to be used and to create unnecessary suffering for civilians and combatants alike, especially in the hostilities in the former Yugoslavia. NGOs working with cluster munition victims as well as certain forward-thinking states continued to believe that cluster munitions caused more harm than provided military benefit, and ought to be prohibited, or at the very least, regulated and restricted in its use. In 1983, a report issued by the United Nations Environment Program described the impact of cluster munitions and recommended the regulation of these weapons, adding to the body of research that condemned the weapons and providing further impetus to the cause. Advocates of a ban believed that the international community should create a new legal instrument that would better regulate cluster munitions and prevent harm to civilians from duds and strikes. The CCW contained a provision to negotiate further protocols for specific categories of weapons and states sought to reach agreement on the cluster munitions issue within this venue.

Explosive Remnants of War and Mines: Banning Individual Weapons

While further progress in restricting the most harmful types of weapons used by both states and non-state groups stalled at the international negotiating table, anti-personnel mines and cluster munitions continued to be used in conflicts worldwide, increasingly over the next few decades. As international attention spotlighted these issues, the pre-cursor to the campaign to ban cluster munitions, namely the Ottawa Process, led by the International Campaign to Ban Landmines (the ICBL), successfully achieved consensus on an international agreement to restrict the use of anti-personnel mines in armed conflict. The Oslo Process echoed in many ways the steps taken in the Ottawa Process a decade earlier, and many lessons learned in that first campaign were applied later. This section describes the landmine ban process as well as the attempts to ban cluster munitions in negotiations undertaken within the umbrella of the United Nations.

Spurred by Victory: The Success of the Landmine Ban

"No other issue in recent times has mobilized such a broad and diverse coalition of countries, governments and nongovernmental organizations (NGOs). Much of this momentum has been the result of the tremendous efforts made by NGOs to advance the cause to ban AP mines. Their commitment and dedication have contributed to the emergence of a truly global partnership."
- Lloyd Axworthy, Minister of Foreign Affairs, Canada, "AP Mine Ban: Progress Report"

Antipersonnel mines were used extensively by both states and non-state armed groups in combat because they were cheap, low-tech and easy to mass produce. They were initially used defensively, to protect strategic areas such as borders, camps or important bridges and to restrict the movement of opposing forces. Land mines are designed to maim rather than kill an enemy soldier, in order to use up more resources of the enemy (which are thus expended in providing care for the wounded soldier).

Over time, antipersonnel landmines began to be adopted on a wider scale, often in internal conflicts and specifically used to target civilians, by terrorizing communities, denying access to farming land and restricting population movement.

While initially mines were mapped to warn people of their presence, they started to be placed strategically in such a way that civilians, aid workers and soldiers had no prior knowledge of the location of a minefield. Often those planting the mines themselves lost track of their locations. Minefields were also impacted by the weather, shifting in such a way as to make detection and clearance almost impossible. Despite technological advancements, land mines continued to cause civilian casualties, since much like in the case of cluster munitions, the so-called technical advancements often failed or were not deployed.

Although the landmine problem had been around for a while, it was not until the late 1980s that the International Campaign to Ban Landmines (ICBL) started to mobilize, after the inclusion of restrictions on the use of anti-personnel mines in the Convention on Conventional Weapons. The use of landmines in armed conflict had increased dramatically during that period. NGO experts decided to collaborate on the landmine issue due to the problems that they posed to humanitarian work, especially since the presence of mines created challenges for reconstruction and development and disproportionately affected rural communities. The ICBL was formally launched in 1992, comprising of six NGOs, two of which, Human Rights Watch and Handicap International, were also instrumental in the cluster munition ban process.

While the ICBL focused its advocacy on calling for a moratorium on the use of anti-personnel mines, other prominent organizations such as the ICRC (International Committee of the Red Cross) merely asked for robust self-destruct mechanisms to be included that would reduce the post-conflict effects of their use. However, within a few years, the discourse from NGOs and even the UN Secretary-General altered towards supporting an outright ban, although without a specific time-frame in mind. An ICRC - sponsored independent review of the military utility of anti-personnel mines concluded potently: "their prohibition and elimination should be pursued as a matter of utmost urgency by governments and the entire international community". Giving a huge fillip to the cause, and echoing the cluster munition ban process, in 1995 Belgium became the first country to nationally ban the use of landmines.

CCW Review Conferences during 1995 and 1996 led to the adoption of the amended Protocol II on the use of mines, booby-traps and other devices. According to Borrie, the amendment unfortunately "fell short of the expectations of many" who had hoped for a comprehensive ban on the use of anti-personnel mines, instead of a ban on the use and transfer of "undetectable" anti-personnel mines and those that failed to self-destruct to a specific standard. Compliance by signatories would moreover not be mandatory for nine years after the entry into force of Protocol II. This watered-down amendment failed to satisfy the expectations of NGOs and observers who had been optimistic about a more comprehensive agreement amidst a changing global political environment.

Many states had publicly expressed their support for a comprehensive ban on landmines, and a small number of states banded together and became more vocal about their support. In October 1996, with the support of these "like-minded states", Canada launched the Ottawa Process, taking ownership of ensuring a global ban on the weapons, and announcing a signing ceremony in Ottawa by December of the next year. Propelled by the core group of interested states and the ICBL, negotiations for this treaty occurred outside the traditional United Nations framework, although supported by various UN field agencies. In December 1997, 122 countries signed the Convention on the Prohibition of the Use, Stockpiling, Production, Transfer of Anti-

Personnel Mines and on Their Destruction (the Mine Ban Treaty). The same year, ICBL and its coordinator Jody Williams received the Nobel Peace Prize as recognition for their work in making the dream of a ban on landmines a reality.

Banning Cluster Munitions Within the CCW: Take Two

Humanitarian concerns have often failed to translate into effective action once they've been put through the lowest-common denominator blender of international negotiations.
– Patricia Lewis, UNIDIR, Oslo Conference

After the success of the landmine ban victory, civil society advocates and states that supported a moratorium on the use of cluster munitions were understandably optimistic about their chances. However, officials and bureaucrats believed that it was an unrepeatable feat, largely brought out about by luck and the endorsement of the late Princess Diana, whose support gave a recognizable face and considerable media attention to the cause of banning anti-personnel mines.

The political winds changed, however, after the extensive use of cluster munitions in campaigns in Kosovo and Afghanistan. During the 1999 NATO campaign in the former Yugoslavia, 10% of all civilian deaths were attributed to unexploded ordnance from cluster bombs used by NATO forces. Due to the media attention following a few particularly high-profile attacks with many civilian casualties, President Clinton suspended the use of cluster munitions during the war. Cluster bombs were also heavily used by the United States in Afghanistan in 2001 - 2002, and in Iraq in 2003 by both Britain and the United States. Conservative estimates report that at least 10,000 unexploded bomblets were left after the close of active hostilities in Afghanistan, and several thousand in Iraq, many used in urban and residential areas.

The increasing use of cluster bombs in large numbers, many of which failed at high rates partially due to the adverse conditions in which they were deployed, as well as more media interest in the casualties caused by these munitions, led to renewed interest in proposing a ban. International human rights organizations tried to use the 2001 CCW meeting to propose a ban on cluster munitions and more regulation. Although they were not particularly optimistic about the conclusion of a successful protocol on cluster munitions, at least initially, NGOs working on the issue believed that the CCW was the best venue to raise awareness and debate the issue. Additionally, even if a specific protocol on cluster munitions was not achieved, which still was the primary objective, even a more generic protocol generally addressing the issue of explosive remnants of war would be an acceptable and more realistic outcome. An ongoing problem that faced the cluster munition ban campaign was the limited resources that were available to be devoted to the problem. Those most knowledgeable and intent on the ban were at the same time focusing their resources on the landmine ban's adoption and implementation.

The International Committee of the Red Cross (ICRC) broached the idea of a protocol specifically dealing with the issues caused by ERW (explosive remnants of war), which gained resonance and a commitment to further discuss the issue. Cluster munitions were discussed only in the context of technical improvements in order to reduce their humanitarian impact. The major users, producers and stockpilers of cluster munitions were against discussing any restrictions at all to the use of the weapons. In 2002 - 2003, during meetings regarding the ERW Protocol, Switzerland tried to get an agreement on greater technical controls on cluster munitions as well as a specific cluster munition protocol. This suggestion was supported by several states including Norway, Austria, Sweden and Canada. However, China, Russia and Pakistan protested against measures that in their view were costly and overly restrictive, and Russia and the United States argued for the adequacy of existing international humanitarian law. These objections effectively tabled all discussion on cluster munitions at the time.

States Parties to the CCW did manage to find consensus generally on the issue of ERW, adopting Protocol V on Explosive Remnants of War on 28 November 2003, which entered into force in November 2006. Article 2 of the Protocol defined unexploded ordnance as "explosive ordnance that has been primed, fused, armed, or otherwise prepared for use and used in an armed conflict. It may have been fired, dropped, launched or projected and should have exploded but failed to do so". Protocol V requires State Parties to take responsibility and provide assistance, "where feasible", towards marking and clearing of explosive ordnance. Article 5 also requires State Parties to take all possible precaution to protect civilians from the effects of explosive remnants of war. Therefore, if cluster bomblets fall under the category of explosive ordnance, Protocol V mandates the responsibility of states to provide clearance and protect civilians from the effects of submunitions from cluster bomb use.

Protocol V reiterated the need for states to take responsibility for post-conflict harm as a result of cluster bomb use, but it did not ban its use or create specific actions for implementation. Additionally, a treaty was specifically needed to explicitly lay out the obligations of State Parties. Whilst the protocol creates some generic obligations for State Parties in addressing the humanitarian concerns associated with explosive remnants, the requirements are not stringent enough, nor are they mandatory. The ICRC highlighted the need to go beyond Protocol V during the Oslo Conference:

The 2003 Protocol on Explosive Remnants of War can play an important role in protecting civilians from unexploded and abandoned ordnance. But it is not, in itself, adequate to address the specific problems and challenges posed by cluster munitions. The Protocol does not contain legally-binding measures to prevent explosive ordnance, including cluster munitions, from becoming explosive remnants of war. The Protocol does not address the high risk of indiscriminate effects from a cluster munitions attack when the submunitions do detonate as intended, particularly if the attack is in a populated area.

However, simply by highlighting the negative effects of cluster munitions, Protocol V strengthened opposition to the weapons and granted an unforeseen fillip to the process. International organizations and the newly formed Cluster Munition Coalition (a group of organizations dedicated towards the prohibition of cluster munitions), continued to push for more stringent measures regarding cluster munitions under the aegis of the CCW. Following Israel's egregious misuse of cluster munitions during its 2006 war against Lebanon, the cries for a more comprehensive protocol increased.

During the Third Review Conference for the CCW, a proposal for negotiating a legally-binding document to address concerns surrounding cluster munitions was signed by thirty states, and it finally appeared as if consensus had been built on this issue. Even UN Secretary-General Kofi Annan sent a message that appeared to urge States Parties towards the logical outcome: "Recent events show that the atrocious, inhumane effects of these weapons—both at the time of their use and after conflict ends—must be addressed immediately, so that civilian populations can start rebuilding their lives. I urge States Parties to the CCW to make full use of this framework to devise effective norms that will reduce and ultimately eliminate the horrendous humanitarian and development impact of these weapons".

Despite the palpable mandate, the major military powers opposed the proposal to negotiate a cluster munition protocol. As Human Rights Watch stated: "The tyranny of consensus doomed the proposal for future cluster munition negotiations in the CCW." Although the proposal was rejected, a number of states issued a declaration on cluster munitions, calling for prohibiting the use of cluster munitions within "concentrations of civilians". On the final day of the conference, Norway announced its intention to start an independent process outside the CCW to negotiate a cluster munitions treaty, thus initiating the Oslo Process.

3

THE OSLO PROCESS

LEVERAGING THE POWER OF THE "MUTUALLY EFFECTIVE PARTNERSHIP"

...[W]e have succeeded because of the partnership of bold and committed governments, the CMC and civil society more broadly, the ICRC, and UN agencies. We have also succeeded because of the vision and determination of many individuals.
- Steve Goose, Cluster Munition Coalition, Oslo Signing Conference

PROGRESS ON AN INTERNATIONAL INSTRUMENT REGULATING THE USE of cluster munitions and mitigating against their effects had stalled for decades. Escalating use of cluster munitions in urban conflicts, with an ever-growing threat of harm to civilians living in the vicinity of such conflicts, motivated states concerned with this intensifying humanitarian problem to take alternative action. This chapter details the events that led to the launch of the Oslo process, its primary drivers and the steps taken that lead to the culmination of a successful agreement on cluster munitions in the summer of 2008.

. . .

Breaking Away From The CCW

We are all here because we have recognized that the impacts of cluster munitions on civilians need to be dealt with effectively and we agree that it is a problem that will require collective action as well as national-level action.

- Patricia Lewis, UNIDIR, Oslo Conference

Lighting the Spark: Israel's 2006 Onslaught

After the disappointment of the CCW's Third Review Conference and the failure yet again to achieve consensus on the issue of cluster munitions, it would have been safe to assume that the topic of banning or regulating the use of cluster munitions would then be relegated to the bottom of the pile of diplomatic priorities, as it had done for decades previously. However, events earlier that year, in the late summer of 2006, ensured that the issue of the harm from the use of cluster munitions and a need to regulate their use would remain on the agenda of the international community.

The catalyst for this urgency and resolve was the extensive use of cluster munitions by Israel in its conflict with Lebanon in July - August 2006. During the 34 day war with Hezbollah, Israel deployed four million submunitions on South Lebanon in over 900 separate strikes. According to the United Nations, over 90% of the cluster munition strikes occurred in the *last three days* of the war, while a settlement was close to being negotiated. Human Rights Watch called the Israeli tactic "saturation cluster bombing", while one Lebanese citizen said more simply, "it started raining cluster bombs". These strikes occurred after the United Nations Security Council had adopted Resolution 1701 on August 11, 2006, calling for an immediate ceasefire, but before officials from the two nations had met to settle the details for the formal cease-fire to take effect on August 14. The settlement, if it took place as was likely, would herald the return of civilians who had fled their homes and villages. Coating the villages and towns with submunition duds ensured that the legacy of the thirty-four day war would remain as a permanent reminder for years, if not decades.

Within months, states as well as international organizations were advocating for re-opening the discussion on an international treaty regulating these weapons. The UN's humanitarian coordinator in Lebanon, David Shearer, said, "The outrageous fact is that nearly all of these [cluster] munitions were fired in the last three to four days of the war.... Outrageous because by that stage the conflict had been largely resolved in the form of [UN Security Council] Resolution 1701". Not only were many states appalled by this egregious display, international organizations such as the United Nations and the ICRC renewed their focus on and interest in working to find a lasting solution to the humanitarian issues caused by the unethical and possibly unlawful use of these harmful weapons. They wanted to ensure that the dubious legality of such use was addressed, and at the very least, an agreement was sought to ensure that the most lethal, oldest and least reliable munitions were prohibited and destroyed, to save another recurrence of the devastating consequences of an unprecedented amount of unexploded ordnance left behind in Lebanon, as it had been in Laos, Cambodia and Vietnam so many decades earlier.

Setting the Stage

At the same time that the United States launched its war on terror in Afghanistan, and later joined forces with the United Kingdom to invade Iraq, negotiations were on between 2001 and 2003 towards an agreement on explosive remnants of war and the use of cluster munitions within the Convention on Conventional

Weapons forum. Cluster munitions had been used widely during both wars, as well as during the 1999 Kosovo conflict, with wide-ranging and documented humanitarian impacts. The two wars in the new century were different from those waged previously, with a blurring of the lines between enemy combatants and civilians, and an increasing amount of combat taking place in residential or mixed-use areas. While in previous decades, these munitions may have been used in traditional battlefield settings, they were now being employed in urban neighborhoods and villages, leaving explosive remnants in backyards, schoolyards and soccer fields, where they killed unsuspecting civilians and exacerbated the devastating effects of war on the populace. NGOs committed to the cause continued to lobby governments to come to an accept-able agreement; however, they were themselves diverted and overwhelmed, also occupied with overseeing the implementation of the landmine ban, enacted in 1997. It was unclear that govern-ments were making significant progress towards a cluster muni-tion ban, and clearly, a more concerted effort on the part of civil society was needed to move the issue forward.

It was decided that a separate organization focused on the goal of banning cluster munitions was necessary. On November 13, 2003, fifteen days before the adoption of Protocol V on the CCW, the Cluster Munition Coalition (CMC) was born. NGOs that had been invited to be part of the process towards Protocol V decided that joining forces and working in concert would garner more positive results, and formed a civil society coalition to push for a ban on cluster munitions. Steve Goose, the co-chairman of the CMC, recalled: "NGOs...decided that the time had come to form a new NGO coalition to carry out more effective work on cluster munitions...it had become very evident that NGOs were mostly operating in emergency response mode on cluster munitions, sounding alarm bells whenever they were used in major conflicts, but that biannual outrage would not suffice. The time had come... to establish expanded, sustained, proactive, and coordinated NGO work on cluster munitions". Throughout 2004 - 2006, the Cluster Munition Coalition worked hard to push for progress on tougher regulations for cluster munitions within the CCW forum, but most states were not committed to anything more substantive than a broad discussion within the context of the problem of explosive remnants of war. However, advocacy on the national level had more success, with Belgium becoming the first country to pass legislation in February 2006 banning cluster munition use. Subsequently, four months later, Norway declared the use of cluster munitions discontinued.

Launching Oslo

By the time the Israel-Lebanon conflict occurred, the Cluster Munition Coalition had already spent a few years lobbying states within the CCW (Convention on Conventional Weapons) process to create a binding agreement regulating and restricting the use of cluster munitions by states. The CCW process was stalled by the interests of military powers that had a vested interest in preserving the status quo. Arguments over the legality and morality of using these weapons had been repeated interminably and the miracles of technologically advanced "smart" munitions that prevented civilian harm were touted by the states who possessed such weapons. Yet it was seen repeatedly that these claims failed in real-world scenarios. Munitions with so-called "self-destruct" capabilities failed to do as advertised, either as a result of improper use (the wrong height or type of soil could change how they performed in actual battle conditions as compared to test sites) or defects in the weapon.

As the death toll from cluster munitions to civilians and the impact on affected countries rose, states that believed these weapons needed to be regulated knew that the CCW process was not the venue to make that happen. Some states like Belgium and Norway (and many more in the months and years to follow) understood the importance and extent of this issue and enacted national laws banning the use of cluster munitions.

Despite these initial victories, most states were not convinced of the need to prohibit cluster munitions, and the prospect of a ban was still quite far off. Then, in 2006, the Lebanon crisis gave the ban process a much-needed impetus. The use of millions of munitions by Israel and the documentation of this offensive by members of the Cluster Munition Coalition provided fodder for action. While the official UN channels failed in getting states to agree on a resolution, the events in Lebanon propelled Norway to take on a leadership role. The Norwegian Minister of Foreign Affairs announced: "This is why Norway will take the lead— together with other like-minded countries and international humanitarian actors—to put in place an international prohibition against cluster munitions". While just weeks earlier it seemed that progress on an international agreement for cluster munitions was an impossibility, seemingly out of nowhere, Norway stepped up to the fray, and like Canada in the case of the Mine Ban Treaty, took on the challenge of spearheading an important and difficult arms control agreement.

Forming the Partnership

This partnership between governments, NGOs, the ICRC and UN agencies is demonstrating that a new diplomacy can work, one built on common interests, that puts the protection of civilians first and foremost.
– Steve Goose, Cluster Munition Coalition Co-Chair, Opening Statement Dublin Conference

The success of negotiating the Convention on Cluster Munitions has been attributed by many experts to the unique collaboration between international organizations, states and civil society. The representative from Austria stated: "The process that brought us here is proof that arms control and disarmament are alive. True, it is a different type of multilateral diplomacy. It is based on a *mutually enriching partnership* involving governments, parliaments, civil society, international organizations, private companies, academics and survivors...This new partnership requires close cooperation and mutual respect, a willingness to listen to each other, a willingness to trust one another. It is new, it is different, but it is successful *(emphasis added)*".

The *mutually enriching partnership* that drove the cluster munition ban campaign had three crucial components: civil society (with the Cluster Munition Coalition at the helm), states that pushed for the ban, and international organizations, in particular, the United Nations and the ICRC. The process was initiated at the Third Review Conference of the CCW, as a response to the lack of progress on the problem of cluster munitions within the framework of the CCW. Norway spearheaded this process, encouraging other states to participate and working in partnership with NGOs and civil society campaigners. In the late fall of 2006, Norwegian Foreign Minister Jonas Gahr Støre announced an international conference to launch the process, stating that "We must take advantage of the political will now evident in many countries to prohibit cluster munitions that cause unacceptable humanitarian harm. The time is ripe to establish broad cooperation on a concerted effort to achieve a ban".

Support From Pro-Ban States

The Oslo process was initiated and given momentum by Norway, who lead the process and dictated the timeline. The process would not also have been successful without a small but committed group of states dubbed the **Core Group of states** (Austria, Ireland, Mexico, New Zealand, Norway, Peru and the Holy See), who spearheaded and lead the Oslo Process, taking turns to host conferences in Oslo, Lima, Vienna, Wellington and Dublin, as well as assisting with regional conferences.

A large number of countries participated in the Oslo Process at various stages. Nations from six continents, both developed and developing countries, supported the process, including over two dozen states affected by cluster munitions, over half the stockpiler states and more than two-thirds of the users and producers of cluster munitions, including the United Kingdom, one of the biggest users of the weapon. Although some of the major military powers (also the biggest detractors of restricting cluster munition use), such as Russia, China, India and the United States did not participate, some experts claim that their absence contributed to a stronger and more humanitarian-centric agreement.

Civil Society and the Cluster Munition Coalition

Aside from states, non-state actors and civil society organizations were a crucial element of the partnership and almost an equal partner in the entire process. Their role was so valuable that even the preamble to the Convention on Cluster Munitions highlights it in the process that led to its creation:

> *Stressing* the role of public conscience in furthering the principles of humanity as evidenced by the global call for an end to civilian suffering caused by cluster munitions and *recognising* the efforts to that end undertaken by the United Nations, the International Committee of the Red Cross, the Cluster Munition Coalition and numerous other non-governmental organisations around the world.

The Cluster Munition Coalition (CMC), the primary civil society body supporting the Oslo Process, was a conglomeration of around 350 NGOs from more than 90 countries, with expertise ranging from disarmament, peace and security, human rights, victim assistance, women's rights and other areas. The steering committee of the CMC was made up of ten NGOs that came together in November 2003 to ban cluster munitions. These organizations represented affected countries, user countries and producer countries, and their collective expertise gave the campaign its edge. Founding members included Human Rights Watch, Handicap International and other leaders from the Nobel Peace Prize-winning International Campaign to Ban Landmines (ICBL), which campaigned towards the 1997 Mine Ban Treaty. The mission of the CMC was to call for "an immediate moratorium on the use of cluster munitions, an acknowledgement of states' responsibility for the explosive remnants they cause, and a commitment to provide resources to areas affected by ERW".

The Cluster Munition Coalition, like the ICBL before it, provided all the elements that the Core Group of states could not themselves bring to the table. Civil society was "the engine that drove the Oslo Process", bringing together expert opinion, victim testimony, documentation and legal analysis throughout the process. Victims of cluster munition attacks attended the conferences, where they made formal statements and added informal interventions from the floor. Their presence constantly reminded the delegates of the humanitarian underpinnings of the issue, and their responsibility to the hundreds of thousands of cluster munition victims in over four decades of its use. Civil society also reached out to citizens, involving them in a bid to further put pressure on their governments. One of their initiatives was driving a "Ban Bus" around Ireland before the Dublin Conference, to spread awareness of the cluster munition ban campaign. Another initiative by the CMC was a global Day of Action in 50 countries in April 2008, to give momentum to the issue before the Dublin conference in May.

At the conferences, civil society representatives lobbied behind-the-scenes and contributed to the discussion at sessions where they were included. One of the reasons that NGOs were so integral to the process was their ability to take a stronger position on the issues, given their independence from states. The CMC lobbied inside and outside the process, often taking the strongest humanitarian position on various issues of contention. This gave pro-ban states political room to maneuver in negotiations with states who were opposed to the ban or on the fence. In a way, the NGOs played the role of the "bad cop", letting states be the "good cop", and preserve their alliances. Their contribution was perceived as so effective in swaying certain states away from military considerations and towards more robust humanitarian provisions that some of the Like-minded group (states who had particularly strong vested military interests), feeling threatened by the efficacy of civil society, petitioned Ireland (the host of the Dublin conference) to exclude them from the discussions at that venue.

The Role of International Organizations

Despite the Oslo Process being parallel to and not officially part of the formal UN channel, the United Nations played a key role in the entire process. The United Nations Development Programme (UNDP) was already present in many of the countries affected by cluster munitions and had well-developed networks with policymakers in these countries. Of the 80 countries worldwide known to be affected by explosive remnants of war, UNDP was present at the time of the Oslo Process in at least 23 of them. Thus, the UNDP was able to contribute "first-hand experience of both the short-term humanitarian impact and the longer term development impact that these munitions have on populations and communities", according to UNDP Bureau for Crisis Prevention and Recovery Chief, Mr. Peter Batchelor. While there were internal conflicts between various departments on the official UN policy regarding cluster munitions, the Lebanon conflict enabled them to come to the same page to some extent, and become supportive of the Oslo process when it launched.

International organizations also provided logistical support to the Oslo process. UNDP was approached by Peru to assist in the preparations for the Lima Conference, for which they provided assistance in capacity-building, information-sharing and in providing a sponsorship program to enable delegates from developing countries and victim spokespersons to participate. The UNDP continued to perform this role in subsequent conferences and helped to organize events in various countries in support of the process, funded in most part by the Core Group countries.

In addition, UNDP worked closely with other UN agencies, providing expertise and knowledge in the form of background papers and briefings. Various UN agencies, including UNICEF, UNDP, and UN Mine Action Service (UNMAS), provided expertise gained from designing and implementing programs addressing various aspects of arms control issues. For instance, United Nations Institute for Disarmament Research (UNIDIR) prepared a draft background paper on cluster munitions for the participants at the Oslo Conference. Their expertise with navigating the intricacies of international advocacy, as well the UNDP's understanding of the needs of development played an important role not only in providing the structure for the process but also by advising its content. The UN also contributed to public relations, including sponsoring an advertisement in the International Herald Tribune meant to draw attention to the dangers of cluster munition use for children.

The UNDP also worked in tandem with the Core Group countries to provide a framework to the process, as well as the backdrop of bureaucracy. The UN and the International

Committee of the Red Cross (ICRC) wholeheartedly supported the Oslo Process, believing that it had a much higher likelihood of success in addressing the issue of cluster munitions.

The International Committee of the Red Cross was seen by states as both a "guardian" of as well as a credible expert on international humanitarian law. In some ways, it had far more credibility with states than NGOs, and as such, their involvement in the Oslo process filled a gap that no one else could, as a source of expertise on the tangible problems with using cluster munitions.

From 2000 onwards the ICRC had been calling for a moratorium on the use of cluster munitions till the problems with that use could be resolved and they were banned from such use in populated areas. The ICRC, much like the UN, was in a difficult position with regard to the Oslo process. They were involved in the CCW process and didn't want to jeopardize either that process or their relationship to it. However, the crisis with cluster munitions in Lebanon in 2006 acted as a spur, and the ICRC recognized that the undertaking embarked on by Norway had a much greater chance of reaching a strong humanitarian outcome. The ICRC strengthened its rhetoric regarding a legal solution to the problem and lent its support openly to the Oslo process. Given the ICRC's credibility, their support of the Oslo process, according to Borrie, "made it easier for some states to justify their participation".

The ICRC contributed to the process by producing a multilingual film, brochures and briefings for delegates, and holding a regional workshop for South-east Asian countries in Bangkok in April 2008. They also organized a media trip for international print, radio and television journalists to a cluster munition affected province in Laos. As stated by a commentator, "...the ICRC and UN positions influenced other participants' views, including those of many governments". The Oslo process would not have been able to achieve its success without the capable and impartial support of the International Committee of the Red Cross and the United Nations.

The Parallel Process

Both processes have the same humanitarian objective. In these circumstances, they should not be seen as in competition with one another but as complementary and mutually reinforcing.
– Ban Ki-Moon, United Nations Secretary-General, Oslo Conference

The developments between 2006 and 2008 towards the achievement of the ban on the use, production, stockpiling and transfer of cluster munitions are collectively called the Oslo Process. The Oslo Process began in 2006 as a fast-track multilateral process towards addressing the humanitarian problems caused by cluster munitions. Beginning with the Oslo Conference in 2007, the parallel process initiated by Norway consisted of a series of conferences that acted as venues for states interested in coming to an agreement on cluster munitions to meet and discuss the various issues involved. The process ended with a final negotiation at Dublin in May 2008. This process continued parallel to negotiations undertaken within the CCW (Convention on Conventional Weapons) forum, where states party to the CCW discussed the issue of submunitions, although that process ultimately failed to reach a satisfactory resolution.

Firing the Starting Pistol: Kicking Off the Negotiations

Representatives from 49 countries, as well as the United Nations, International Committee of the Red Cross and the

Cluster Munition Coalition, participated in the Oslo Conference on Cluster Munitions on February 22 - 23, 2007, kicking off the discussions on banning cluster munitions. The goal of the Oslo Conference was to start off the proceedings, to set the ball rolling as it were, and over time to "gather [a] critical mass" of support from a wider group of states. Not all states, especially those outside the Core Group, were comfortable with the idea of such a conference; however, some felt that it would be better to attend and have a chance to at least influence the outcome, not to mention the optics of being seen as caring about the issue. The participation of the United Kingdom especially was crucial, since that gave further legitimacy to the conference, and made it easier for other NATO members to attend. While the Oslo Conference was clearly intended as a kick-off to a parallel process to the CCW negotiations, some of the states, including the UK, wanted to pretend otherwise, and maintain the notion, at least early in the proceedings, that there was no intent to compete with the CCW diplomatic process.

Norway, taking the lead on this conference and the entire process, wanted to accomplish three things by the end of the Oslo Conference: 1) obtain a clear political commitment from governments, 2) ensure that the commitment was communicated in terms conducive to media and PR coverage, and 3) create agreement on concrete next steps. The stated purpose of the conference was "to raise awareness of the urgent need for states to address the problems caused by cluster munitions". Speakers at the conference included Norwegian diplomatic officials, members of civil society organizations and the Cluster Munition Coalition, and most crucially, survivors of cluster munition attacks. The presence of the latter reminded the participants of the humanitarian underpinnings of the issue.

At this early point in the process, there was surprisingly little agreement, even within and among the partners, on either strategy or tactics going forward. There was a debate within the

Cluster Munition Coalition for instance, on how to strategically position their message and viewpoint; while initially, the process didn't explicitly seek to ban *all* cluster munitions, it was clear that would be the necessary end goal. The challenge for the CMC was presenting this goal to states who were more comfortable with the idea of a selective ban while preserving at the same time, their position as a staunchly humanitarian organization as well as a trusted advisor and partner to all states. In the end, a compromise was reached, with the CMC calling for "the conclusion of an international treaty banning cluster munitions by 2008", with no mention of any sub-categories of weapons or other specifics.

The tight deadline (of a day and a half), and the reluctant participation of certain states notwithstanding, the Oslo Conference ended with a firm endorsement by 46 governments (out of the 49 states who attended) to conclude by 2008 "a legally binding international instrument that will: (i) prohibit the use, production, transfer and stockpiling of cluster munitions that cause unacceptable harm to civilians, and (ii) establish a framework for cooperation and assistance that ensures adequate provision of care and rehabilitation to survivors and their communities, clearance of contaminated areas, risk education and destruction of stockpiles of prohibited cluster munitions". Only three states had declined to join the declaration – Japan, Poland and Romania – and far more had endorsed it than even the organizers had hoped for. While many concerns remained, such as the important questions of which types of cluster munitions if any would be banned and the feasibility of keeping the discussions outside the official channels, these were tabled for future conferences. Despite the inevitable hiccups, the Oslo Conference was a resounding success because the process was under way, a firm declaration had been made, and the path forward was already laid out.

Keeping Up the Momentum: Gaining Supporters For the Ban

The goal at the conclusion of the Oslo Conference was to include a wider and more global participation in the process, from all regions of the world. This goal was accomplished via further global and regional conferences, to keep the discussions open and the momentum going forward. Throughout 2007 and 2008 there were subsequent conventions in Cambodia, Costa Rica, Serbia, Belgium, Zambia, Laos and Lebanon among others, during which the provisions of the treaty were parsed out by participating governments. Additionally, regional meetings were held to encourage states to join the Oslo Process and gain a better understanding of the aims of the treaty. Although awareness of the issues was increasing, there was still no real consensus between states on the provisions of the agreement.

Lima: The First Major Conference

During the Lima Conference (May 23 - 25, 2007), states discussed substantive aspects of the draft convention. The Lima conference focused on discussions centered around the humanitarian provisions of the intended agreement - victim assistance, clearance of unexploded ordnance, stockpile destruction - and attempted to devote as little time as possible towards a debate over definitions. Many of the substantive discussions at this conference were the precursors to the humanitarian provisions that ultimately formed the bedrock of the treaty text. The number of states participating at the Lima conference increased from 49 (at Oslo) to 68, many from Africa, Asia and Latin America.

Two noteworthy aspects of the discussion at Lima concerned a single exclusion of cluster munitions with submunitions that engage point targets, which led to a discussion on other possible exclusions; and additionally, the inclusion into the draft of a provision on victim assistance.

Germany proposed a draft CCW protocol on cluster munitions after the signing of the Oslo Declaration (at the ICRC experts' meeting); one that was not met with favorably by most states given the timing of the proposal and the increased expectations and hopes of most states for a more robust agreement. However, it illustrated the significant differences in approach among the various states who were even willing to negotiate the issue of cluster munitions, and as Borrie states, it illuminated the difficult road ahead.

Vienna: No "Good" Submunitions

The next significant conference was the Vienna conference, held on December 5 - 7, 2007. In the intervening period, to maintain momentum and increase the support for the treaty, regional meetings were held on a smaller scale, in Costa Rica, Jordan and Belgrade. Additionally, during the celebrations for the 10th anniversary of the Mine Ban Treaty adoption in Oslo, the Norwegian government lobbied states present to back the emerging Oslo process, linking together the issues of landmines and cluster munitions.

Initially, early in the process, it was assumed by many states, that the agreement would end up banning only certain types of munitions, the most harmful, which were deemed the ones with the highest failure rates. The UK called them "dumb cluster munitions", a misnomer as the very nature of cluster munitions meant that there could be no "smart cluster munitions". Borrie argues that the shift away from the focus on certain types of weapons coincided with the participation of more states, especially those who had experienced first-hand the effects of the use of these weapons and were more vested in mitigating these effects rather than preserving the military advantages of states who stockpiled cluster bombs. Many of the newly participating states, mostly those that did not stockpile the weapon and had not used them in the past, "did not see why all cluster munitions should not be banned as a matter of principle, as anti-personnel mines were".

The definition of cluster munitions in the draft discussion text distributed three weeks before the Vienna conference was far more robust than the one introduced in Lima. The ICRC experts' meeting held in April 2007 served to clarify many of the technical and substantive issues regarding the problems with using cluster munitions, including those that were generally deemed "safer" and less harmful. Although agreement on cluster munition definitions was tabled for later conferences, one thing that emerged during the discussions in Vienna was a clear sense that there was no such thing as less harmful cluster munitions or a meaningful distinction between "good" and "bad" submunitions.

Consensus also emerged at the Vienna Conference on provisions regarding victim assistance, stockpiles, clearance and international cooperation. Concerns regarding certain issues were also raised in Vienna. Key amongst these was the question of 'interoperability', regarding the legality of State Parties collaborating on humanitarian missions with states not party to the agreement, most notably the United States. It was also during this time that the "Like-minded group" emerged, mainly NATO members and allies of the United States, who wanted to maintain their military capabilities and yet be part of the Oslo process and work towards a humanitarian outcome. One of the primary considerations for the group was how to balance their concerns over interoperability (likely fanned by the US) without appearing to be uncooperative in the process, due to media and political pressure. It was at Vienna too that the provision was included in the draft text, requiring past users of cluster munitions to provide humanitarian assistance to affected states. Delegates from 138 states and representatives from 50 countries attended the Vienna Conference, nearly double the number of Lima, illustrating the momentum being built by the Oslo Process. As Borrie stated, "the legitimacy of the Oslo process in humanitarian terms was now beyond serious challenge…"

. . .

Wellington: Drawing Battle Lines

The final major conference before formal negotiations in Dublin took place in Wellington, New Zealand, on February 18 - 22, 2008. There were many additional states that attended this session that were new to the process (including several from the Pacific region), adding to the growing consensus about the relevance of the process and the issue. This was also the most contentious conference, where the issues were debated heatedly, perhaps with a growing sense of urgency as states knew the process was heading towards a conclusion. The Like-minded group of countries (consisting of Australia, Canada, Czech Republic, Denmark, Finland, France, Germany, Italy, Japan, the Netherlands, Slovakia, Sweden, Switzerland, and the United Kingdom) submitted proposals that were criticized by the CMC and others as weakening the text of the treaty. These proposals included exceptions to the types of cluster munitions prohibited, an inclusion of a transition period and provisions on interoperability.

In the first few months of 2008, parallel negotiations were also undertaken on the issue of cluster munitions in the CCW, in part due to the galvanization of opinion on the subject by the Oslo process. The CCW process, although with less ambitious humanitarian objectives, attempted to influence the outcome of the Oslo process by being the first to agree on key terminology. Due to the impracticality of competing sets of definitions, those in the Oslo process would be constrained by the terms emerging from the CCW. Realizing this, the Like-minded group were attempting, according to Borrie, to use the CCW forum as leverage to get better terms in the Oslo process. Thus there appeared to be a back-and-forth approach between the CCW and Oslo negotiations, between the states wanting to preserve safeguards and those wanting a strong humanitarian outcome. The existence of the Oslo process itself served as a catalyst for more serious discussions on cluster munitions, which was previously missing from the CCW.

The Wellington conference was supposed to be a turning point. Till this stage in the process, the conferences were venues for discussion, for the sharing of expertise by civil society representatives, and a way to reiterate the humanitarian aspects of the proposed convention. The conference held in New Zealand in February would mark a change; the goal was to decide the way forward towards the final negotiations in Dublin. There were concerns about the widening gap between the states who wanted no exclusions or exemptions or diluting of the issue in any way, and the Like-minded group, who were lobbying for exceptions and delays.

The Wellington conference was also the first time that the Oslo process was in danger of being derailed completely by the vested interests of a few states. At this conference, the battle lines appeared to be drawn between those who had used cluster munitions (primarily developed nations), and those who had suffered from its use (primarily developing nations). The Like-minded were afraid of either being railroaded by the Core Group and public perception into signing a treaty that would be untenable for them to uphold or having to refrain from the process and bear the aftermath of outrage from both the media and the other states who were prepared to reach a successful conclusion to the process. The affected and non-user states continued to be in favor of the current text, without the additional weakening provisions.

This was a period of high tension on all sides. While the Core Group and civil society had decided that waiting till the final conference in Dublin for substantial negotiations was the right strategy to ensure a stronger humanitarian outcome, the Like-minded states, afraid of not getting their concerns addressed, pushed to get their way at the Wellington conference itself. The Like-minded group were more cohesive and better organized at the Wellington conference than at previous fora, and as Borrie stated in *Unacceptable Harm*, "it soon became apparent in Wellington that the Like-minded had come to the meeting determined to shape the text straight away and not to wait until Dublin". This lead to a fractured atmosphere and behind-the-scenes lobbying as well as outright shaming by certain civil society representatives. "The lack of tact of some of these efforts left others unimpressed, especially among the many developing and cluster munition-affected countries attending the Wellington conference. These countries were alarmed that the Like-minded could weaken the draft convention text for the Dublin negotiations".

As a compromise, the draft text along with the additional proposals submitted by various states (mostly from the Like-minded group) was designated as the starting point for the Dublin negotiations. The proposals also included the progress made regarding articles on clearance and victim assistance during the Wellington conference. Skillful negotiations and tradecraft from members of the Core Group enabled the for-the-first-time- shaky process to continue towards Dublin without major defections from NATO member states.

In the end, 82 states endorsed the Wellington Declaration (with the number of endorsements rising to 111 in the following months), which among other points, committed states to using its text as a starting point in the negotiations in Dublin. As Borrie stated: "A highly ambitious draft convention text was now in place for the Dublin diplomatic conference, along with rules for that negotiation and a strong political reaffirmation of the humanitarian goals of the Oslo process".

In the months leading up to the Dublin negotiations, significant progress was made at regional fronts. Forty African states signed the Livingstone Declaration in Zambia in support of the Oslo Declaration. Mexico hosted a conference in Mexico City on 16 - 17 April 2008, of 22 Latin American and Caribbean states. CMC coordinated a Global Day of Action on 19 April 2008 in 50 countries to highlight the humanitarian impact of cluster munition use. In the aftermath of the contentious Wellington conference, the Cluster Munition Coalition learned important lessons, which they would implement during the final Dublin negotiations. They became more organized and planned more thoroughly for Dublin, including designating roles and specific responsibilities for every member of their delegation, using their campaigners for lobbying, public demonstrations, and liaising with the media. This final conference was the last chance to ensure a strong treaty outcome and create lasting change for the current and future victims of cluster munitions.

Taking It Home: The Final Negotiations

The Dublin Diplomatic Conference from May 19 - 30, 2008 hosted the formal negotiations for the Convention on Cluster Munitions. The conference in Dublin took place at Croke Park, a sports stadium a little outside the city. One hundred and twenty-seven states attended the Dublin Conference, 107 as participants, and 20 as observers. There was a strong showing from civil society - with 284 campaigners (from 61 countries), including a dozen survivors of cluster munition attacks, as part of the Cluster Munition Coalition delegation. CMC delegates lobbied governments on specific treaty provisions, as well as held public events to garner support for a strong Convention. The overwhelming attendance and support no doubt contributed to the successful adoption of the treaty.

In the End Zone: The Consultations at Croke Park

The basis for discussions at Dublin was the draft Wellington conference text, containing a preamble and 22 substantive articles. Despite a constructive atmosphere and a stated commitment to reach agreement on the issues, states differed on many specific points during the Dublin negotiations. Some of the main issues that needed to be agreed upon included the definition of cluster munitions, a transition period before the treaty terms entered into force, the retention of munition stocks for training purposes, and interoperability or joint military operations with non-signatories. Issues on stockpile destruction, transparency and clearance also needed to be settled. All of this moreover had to be accomplished within 8 or 9 days, to enable sufficient time for last-minute negotiations, as well as official translations before the final meeting of states to vote on adopting the treaty.

The Dublin conference was spearheaded by Ireland, not the Core Group. While there were strong or weak alliances at the previous conferences, at Dublin the various groupings weakened a bit, with the exception of the states from Africa, Latin America and other developing countries, who took a stronger humanitarian position on most of the provisions discussed and had developed a united bond in the regional conferences held in the previous months before Dublin. They have been described as the **Tee-total states**, in the sense that they objected to the retention of any munitions, exclusions, transition period or provision on interoperability. Civil society, especially the CMC, helped these states articulate their positions and provided sophisticated counter-arguments during consultations on the substantive issues, through briefings, position papers and other expertise.

In Dublin, the CMC focused their attention on providing behind-the-scenes expertise to states with stronger humanitarian positions, as well as mounted a sophisticated media and public relations campaign. They lobbied politicians, supplied information to the press, undertook public demonstrations and uploaded campaign information in the form of videos online, taking advantage of the platform of new media. They also assigned key members of their leadership team to each of the important issues, facilitating and working with governments to ensure positive outcomes on each crucial article.

It was apparent that their relentless lobbying was reaching its mark. "There were signs too that some states were feeling significant domestic political pressure to promote a successful outcome in Dublin, in good part because of the lobbying efforts of the CMC and its members". Public perception regarding the issue was an important element in informing the policy of some states who might otherwise have preferred a less robust outcome. In the UK, civil society engaged and created relationships with prominent politicians, to ensure Britain's support of the process. A poll conducted in the UK shortly before the final conference showed that nearly 80% of those polled supported the United Kingdom signing the cluster munition treaty, and 50 percent stated that failing to do so would disappoint them. The issue and Britain's stance on it also garnered significant domestic and international media attention, especially because they were a NATO member, a close ally of the United States, and had produced, stockpiled and used cluster munitions. Their support of the new convention would send a strong signal regarding its legitimacy and contribute to its success.

A Full-Court Press: Achieving Agreement on Contentious Provisions

It was clear early on during the negotiations that transition periods wouldn't be acceptable to an overwhelming majority of states. Even while the conference was underway, several states made announcements of their intent towards progress on the issue.

The next most important issue and one with a wide number of viewpoints was regarding the definition of what constituted a cluster munition. This was crucial, as the breadth of the definition would determine how many of the states, especially those with large cluster munitions arsenals, felt equal to adopting the treaty. Many of these states also produced these munitions, and they too would be affected. The consultations on the issue of definitions presided over by Ambassador Don MacKay included the views and participation of all states as well as observers including civil society and the UN. There were many differing positions on the issues, but over the course of the week of discussions, a draft text was agreed on, that attempted to provide a definition that banned almost all of the weapons that acted with the impact of a cluster munition. As Steve Goose from the Cluster Munition Coalition later stated, "If it functions like a cluster munition, it is a cluster munition, and is therefore banned". This was seen widely as a diplomatic coup for the Irish team leading the conference as well as the Oslo process as a whole, as this was a far stronger stance than had been possible through the CCW process.

The other primary sticking point and matter of some contention among the various ideological groupings was the topic of interoperability. For many states, especially NATO members and US allies, the issue of liability for joint operations was an especially important one to settle during the negotiations. During the Dublin conference, the Swiss Ambassador and head of the Swiss delegation to Oslo was asked to lead the discussions on interoperability. Over a week at Croke Park, the various delegations that were most invested in the issue thrashed out their concerns and attempted to come to a decision on how to address it within the text of the treaty. Article 1 of the text stated the general scope and application of the treaty: "each State Party undertakes never under any circumstances to: (a) Use cluster munitions; (b) Develop, produce, otherwise acquire, stockpile, retain or transfer to anyone, directly or indirectly, cluster munitions; (c) Assist, encourage or induce anyone to engage in any activity prohibited to a State Party under this Convention". Concerns from civil society and the Tee-total states related specifically to the provision 1 (c), on "assisting, encouraging or inducing", as they were worried that including exceptions in this first article would severely water down the treaty text and create a giant loophole for States Parties to be able to continue to use cluster munitions.

It was ultimately decided in the course of negotiations to leave in the strong scope of Article 1, and include an additional article at the end dealing with interoperability (Article 21). While most developing nations and the members of civil society present, in particular, the Cluster Munition Coalition, expressed grave concerns about the inclusion of this article, it was clear that many of the NATO members were unable to secure agreement from their governments to endorse the treaty without this assurance. The CMC fought till the last moment, hours before the states were to declare their intentions regarding the agreement, for changes to the wording that they deemed would provide clarity and reduce the negative impact to the overall agreement from the insertion of this additional provision. While the CMC failed to gain these last-minute changes, they realized that they had nevertheless won their over-arching objective - a comprehensive and strong agreement on cluster munitions.

By the end of the Dublin conference, states were more prepared to find a mutually acceptable solution, and the position of many states shifted on contentious issues during or just before the negotiations. As Borrie stated, "...it soon became strikingly apparent that virtually all of the participating states...genuinely sought to achieve a treaty". The final Convention differed significantly from the Wellington treaty text; the former was four pages longer and included an additional article on interoperability.

Despite the tense negotiations of the process and the rollercoaster ride from Oslo to Dublin, the delegations present were proud to be part of such a historic moment and gave impassioned speeches praising the outcome of the Oslo Process. As one observer subsequently commented: "The emotional atmosphere of the Dublin conference's final day was certainly not an artificial bonhomie; even the most taciturn diplomatic negotiators seemed genuinely affected at the new international legal standard they had played their parts in achieving". Although there was a wide range of positions on various issues, by May 30, all 107 participating states were enough in agreement to formally adopt the

2008 Convention on Cluster Munitions. The Dublin conference represented a major landmark in the fight to mitigate the harmful effects of explosive remnants of war on civilians, achieving the endorsement of a large number of countries despite the refusal of many of the major producers and consumers of cluster munitions to be part of the process.

The Oslo Process managed to accomplish within a remarkably short time what years of protracted negotiations within the CCW process had been unable to achieve. "By setting a deadline for completion of their work, defining clear goals at the outset, and dispensing with the constraints of consensus, states were able to keep to a strict timeline and to maintain high standards". The conclusion to the Oslo Process was the Convention on Cluster Munitions Signing Conference at Oslo from December 3 - 4, 2008. Ninety-four states signed the Convention, while four states signed and ratified simultaneously: Norway, Ireland, the Holy See and Sierra Leone. Additionally, 28 countries participated as observers, with many voicing their support to the Convention.

The signing of the cluster munition treaty was, in the words of Oslo's Foreign Minister Jonas Store, a "historic event as it places humanitarian disarmament at the centre stage of international affairs". Utilizing a partnership between affected and non-affected states, the United Nations and the Cluster Munition Coalition, the campaign succeeded in creating the "first international treaty to ban an entire category of conventional weapons". The treaty was coincidentally signed on the anniversary of the Mine Ban Treaty, which marked the first instance of a successful partnership between states and civil society in achieving humanitarian objectives in international law.

4

CONTENTION AND CONTROVERSY
OPPOSITION TO THE OSLO PROCESS

Cooperating on the basis of self-interest toward mutual benefit is the best basis for any coalition, and the best antidote to mistrust."
– Patricia Lewis, UNIDIR, Oslo Conference

THE CONVENTION ON CLUSTER MUNITIONS IS HISTORIC BECAUSE the ban came about despite the adamant opposition by states using, producing and stockpiling cluster munitions. The ban has been primarily opposed on the grounds that cluster munitions are an essential part of the military toolkit, and the best approach towards safeguarding civilian lives is to control the use and sale of these weapons and focus on improving the existing technology available, as well as to contribute to post-conflict clearance of the affected areas.

Understandably, states that have been vested in producing or stockpiling millions of cluster munitions as crucial components of their military arsenals, were extremely unwilling to entertain the financial and strategic cost to their defense capabilities in the event of a complete embargo on these deadly and versatile weapons. Most of the major global military powers adamantly opposed the ban, blocking it during official discussions and lobbying against it during unofficial negotiations.

The primary opponents towards the ban are also coincidentally users and producers of cluster munitions, and also non-signatories of the landmine ban. The countries in this list include the United States, Israel, Russia, China, India and Pakistan. These states not only objected to the ban, in some cases even undermined the Convention by lobbying behind the scenes to prevent its completion, or at the very least, to water down its effectiveness. The United States attempted to prevent its allies and fellow NATO members as well as states tied to and politically dependent on the US such as Afghanistan and Iraq from joining the treaty, albeit unsuccessfully. The New York Times reported in an article on the signing of the Convention that Afghanistan's President Hamid Karzai had bucked pressure from the United States to oppose the cluster munition ban. As the article stated, "The decision appeared to reflect Mr. Karzai's growing independence from the Bush administration, which has opposed the treaty and, according to a senior Afghan official who spoke on the condition of anonymity following diplomatic protocol, had urged Mr. Karzai not to sign it."

The opposition of the countries mentioned above is significant, most importantly that of the US, an important player in the international system. The United States, a major military power and also a veteran user, producer and stockpiler of cluster munitions (having used them in its armed conflicts since the Vietnam War), was opposed to the notion of a ban on cluster munitions from its inception. This is hardly surprising since the United States is also not a signatory to the Mine Ban Treaty, and other humanitarian legislation, most notably the Convention on the Rights of the Child. Militarily and politically an important state, the United States wields extensive influence over decisions on global affairs. Understanding the extent of the objections of the

US and other states towards the ban thus further brings to light the significance of the success of the Oslo Process.

The opponents of a treaty banning the use of cluster bombs had several objections, which can be grouped under five major concerns. States that had used or produced, and continued to stockpile cluster munitions, considered these weapons a significant part of their existing military strategy, and were unwilling to face the costs of replacing these weapons within their arsenals. Additionally, many states objected to cluster munitions being singled out for a ban, as they argued that they were merely a subset of the larger category of explosive remnants of war, the use of which was already restricted and controlled under international law. After the launch of the Oslo Process, which was a process that was parallel to, but outside, the United Nations framework, many states objected to the venue and means of the ban discussion, honing in on the perceived unsanctioned nature of the process. Many states also raised objections and brought proposals throughout the process to create exceptions and include provisions that would benefit them, but would water-down the intent of the treaty. Finally, states were concerned about their ability to engage in joint military operations with allies who may possess cluster munitions. This chapter expands on and assesses each of these objections in greater detail.

Importance of Cluster Munitions to Military Strategy

Essential to the Military Toolkit: Objections of States to the Ban

These weapons may still be considered useful from a narrow battlefield perspective, although many doubt it. But their humanitarian and

political consequences - long after the conflicts have ended - by far
outweigh their usefulness.
– Jonas Gahr Støre, Oslo Conference

The ban was primarily opposed on the grounds that cluster munitions are an essential part of the military toolkit, and as its detractors argued, the best approach towards safeguarding civilian lives
is instead to control the use and sale of these weapons and focus
on improving the existing technology available. One of the
primary objections of many states to banning cluster munitions,
especially those with significant defense capabilities and a
guarded approach to humanitarian legislation, continues to be the
importance of these weapons to their military strategy and arsenal. This section highlights the concerns of a few of those states.

One of the primary objections of the United States to banning
cluster munitions continues to be the importance of these
weapons to their military strategy and arsenal. One author wrote
about the US objection to banning anti-personnel mines: "The
prevailing view of why the United States remained opposed to a
ban [on landmines] is that the US military was firmly wedded to
landmines". The same reason applied to their resistance to the
cluster munitions ban: according to their Acting Assistant Secretary of State for Political-Military Affairs, the US' primary opposition to the ban remains that they rely on cluster bombs as an
important part of their own defense strategy and that many of
their allies rely on them as well.

At the 2007 CCW Review Conference, the Indian ambassador
stated that cluster munitions "offer distinct military advantages
over other munitions in terms of economy of effort and wider
area coverage in combat zones". India also stated at another CCW
meeting, that until cluster munitions could be replaced with other
alternatives which were cost effective and equally effective mili-

tarily, these weapons would continue to be an important part of their military arsenal.

Another military power Brazil, although an observer at many of the conferences as part of the Oslo Process, declined to support the cluster munition ban, stating that cluster munitions were still effective militarily and that it was impractical to try to ban them outright. Brazil stated that "negotiations must include all interested actors, and not just take away weapons from those who do not have them". It asserted that "cluster munitions are effective militarily and that it is not realistic to pretend that they will be eliminated". They also stated at a CCW meeting in November 2008 that "the process and convention [on cluster munitions] did not balance legitimate defense needs with humanitarian concerns".

Finland was one of the countries which despite participating throughout the Oslo Process, ultimately decided to not sign the Convention. Their Minister of Defense stated Finland's reservations: "cluster munitions play an important role in the credibility [and] autonomy...of Finnish defense". They cited the financial costs of replacing their stockpile with alternative weapons, as well as security concerns in its border with Russia for its unwillingness to sign the treaty.

Cambodia was an "early, prominent, and influential supporter" of the cluster munition ban process, being the first country to sign the Oslo Declaration, delivering a keynote address at the Lima conference and affirming that "the Oslo Process was the only way to find the most effective solution to the humanitarian problems caused by cluster munitions". As a country that had suffered firsthand from these humanitarian issues, they supported the process knowing the need for such an important agreement. However, Cambodia failed to sign the convention in 2008, citing "recent security developments in the region", and that it needed more time to study the "impacts of the convention on its security capability and national defense". In 2011, during its border conflict with Thailand, the latter reportedly used cluster munitions against Cambodia. Despite their initial support of the Convention, it is now unclear whether this incident will further strengthen Cambodia's stance against cluster munitions or erode it, perceiving them as a potentially necessary military tool.

Russia is another militarily powerful state that objected to banning cluster munitions due to the ban's impact on its military arsenals. It was additionally only willing to discuss proposals that would allow it to maintain its existing defense capabilities, that would not have any economic implications for Russia, and would focus on regulating the use of cluster munitions and not create technical restrictions.

Military Effectiveness of Cluster Munitions

Cluster munitions are militarily valuable because a) a smaller arsenal is needed to attack multiple targets, as each munition has a large footprint; and b) it enables a smaller unit to take on a larger enemy force. The United States has been historically the largest user of cluster munitions, in campaigns ranging from the Vietnam War, Grenada and Lebanon in 1983, the first Gulf War in 1991, the Yugoslavia conflict in 1999, and most recently, between 2001 - 2003, in Afghanistan and Iraq. Human Rights Watch reported in 2001 that there were over one billion individual submunitions in the United States' military arsenal. Their ground forces possess around 88% of their total stockpiles.

The United States asserts that cluster munition use allows them to reduce the number of aircraft and artillery systems they need to maintain, and eliminating these munitions would put a strain on the resources of the military, as new weapons systems and ammunition would be needed. According to the former Secretary of Defense Robert M. Gates: "The US did not participate in the Cluster Munitions Convention negotiations because we believe that cluster munitions *are an integral part* of our and many of our coalition partners' military operations. The elimination of cluster munitions from our stockpiles would put the lives of our soldiers and those of our coalition partners at risk. There are no substitute munitions, and some of the possible alternatives could actually increase the damage that results from an attack (emphasis added)."

The main argument against the cluster munition ban by Secretary of Defense Gates, therefore, is that the weapons are irreplaceable militarily. On the other hand, Acting Assistant Secretary of State for Political-Military Affairs Robert Mull stated: "We think that it is going to be impossible to ban cluster munitions, as many in the Oslo process would like to do, because these are weapons that have a *certain military utility and are of use* (emphasis added)". It appears therefore that Mull is suggesting that cluster munitions cannot be banned solely because the weapons have a "certain military utility", and their discontinuance would be inconvenient for the US. It may appear to be simply the use of different terminology, but here it is crucial to note that the position against the ban was based on the rationale that the weapons were "integral" and that "there are no substitute munitions".

There is, however, dissent both within and outside the armed services about whether cluster munitions are really essential to the military arsenal. Cluster munitions are more useful in traditional battlefields when facing an invading army or fighting an enemy military that is concentrated in one spot. However, as stated by Norway's Deputy Minister of Defence, Mr. Espen Barth-Eide, "Conflicts worldwide show that cluster munitions, an area weapon originally designed for use against military targets located in open spaces, [are] in fact extensively being used in populated areas". The shift in the nature of warfare dictates the need for the use of more humanitarian alternatives. The wars in Iraq and Afghanistan were often fought extensively in civilian areas, leading to the use of cluster bombs proving fatal to civilians both during the actual attack and then afterward, when civilians come upon the unexploded ordnances.

Not only are cluster munitions more dangerous for civilians, their use also endangers the lives of the soldiers using these weapons. As Mr. Barth-Eide stated, "the use of munitions that are inaccurate or leave large numbers of unexploded ordnance after use may also cause significant problems for the military forces themselves". In Iraq, the use of cluster bombs by Coalition forces impeded their movement and led to some United States' soldiers calling for an end to the use of these weapons. Therefore, far from assisting military objectives, cluster munitions' use can impede these objectives, by increasing costs and injury to personnel and reducing efficiency. As declared by Norway's Deputy Minister of Defence:

> As our Generals tell us, the use of inaccurate or malfunctioning munitions in a military operation means having to spend more ammunition to achieve a given military objective. This implies reduced efficiency, increased costs, as well as increased risks to your own personnel, who may be forced to spend more time in an area before the military aim is achieved, thus making the unit more vulnerable for counter-attack. Additionally, causing large numbers of unexploded ordnance on the ground may also constitute a significant risk to your own personnel and reduce mobility if there is a need to move through the contaminated area at a later stage.

Using weapons that cause unnecessary and disproportionate harm to civilians during conflict can also negate any potential goodwill or humanitarian motives of the military mission. In Kosovo, the humanitarian intervention came under fire when cluster munitions missed their intended military targets and landed on civilian areas, killing hundreds of women and children. As Mr. Barth-Eide stated, "the use of cluster munitions that cause enormous humanitarian problems both during and after the conflict may in fact undermine the overall (political) aim of the military operation."

With the advent of precision-guided munitions, the military necessity of cluster bombs seems more uncertain. While in Operation Desert Storm in 1991, only 10% of weapons used was precision-guided, in the 2003 invasion of Iraq, almost 90% were smart weapons. Thus, not only do alternatives to the use of these weapons exist, states are already using these alternatives.

Technological Fixes: Adopting an Arms Control Approach

"Technical improvements to cluster munitions remained the solution in which the US government preferred to put its faith, rather than new international rules or regulations on the weapon"
– John Borrie

The United States' proposed solution to reduce the humanitarian impact of cluster munitions is to "pursue technological fixes that will make sure that these weapons are no longer viable once the conflict is over". The US focused on technical measures to improve the reliability and accuracy of the weapons—steps that also made cluster munitions more appealing from a military perspective. In 2001, then Secretary of Defense William Cohen issued a policy memorandum stating that all submunitions produced in 2005 onwards must have a failure rate of less than 1%. While this policy did not affect the existing stockpiles of hundreds of millions of submunitions, it could potentially reduce significantly the number of submunitions left behind, and thus the harm to civilians post-conflict.

The United States has argued that the solution would be to work on improving the existing technology, and mandate that only those munitions that have a 99% reliability rate should be allowed to be deployed. However, this failure rate is only achievable in laboratory conditions and does not take into account conditions of use such as faulty delivery technique, the landing of the munitions in a soft or muddy ground or other damage that raises the failure rate. Additionally, when a few million munitions are deployed in battle, even the 99% reliability rate would mean that, due to the large numbers (sometimes millions) of weapons that are deployed at a time, thousands of submunitions would still fail, creating the same humanitarian problems previously stated. In urban warfare, these munitions are often deployed in dual-use areas, where civilians and combatants live or work in close proximity (for instance in the conflicts in Iraq, Afghanistan, Lebanon and Syria). In these instances, a low failure rate would still potentially cause hundreds of civilian casualties, as the submunitions would be spread around an urban and densely populated area. It is also worth noting here that in such cases, the weapons are arguably being used in violation of international humanitarian law, as one of its primary tenets requires states to differentiate between combatants and non-combatants during active conflict.

Thus, as stated by foreign policy expert Leon Sigal, the arms control approach has "severe shortcomings in that it assumes that all actors in fact abide by the rules regulating the use of weapons and that this will indeed spare civilians". At a time of precision weapons, 'dumb' weapons such as cluster munitions are losing their relevance. It has also been predicted by the 2008 National Defence Strategy, that the focus of the US military will be on preparing for missions more like Iraq, where the need for counter-insurgency measures will be greater. Given that the use of cluster munitions was suspended in Iraq and Afghanistan, it is likely that cluster munitions will continue to lose their utility in the United States' overall military strategy.

. . .

Cluster Munitions as a Subset of Explosive Remnants of War

Use Existing IHL and CCW Framework

Some states, in most cases those who were either users or producers of cluster munitions, argued that the regulations that existed under international law were sufficient to deal with the humanitarian issues that stemmed from the use of cluster munitions. China, in its objections to the Convention on Cluster Munitions, despite not having ratified Protocol V of the CCW which deals with explosive remnants, took the position that the existing international humanitarian law and CCW protocols were adequate to address the issue, and there was no need for further international instruments on this subject. At the CCW Group of Governmental Experts session in Geneva in 2005, China stated that "the ERW Protocol has covered general generic preventative measures aimed at improving the reliability of munitions, which will be conducive to addressing the humanitarian problems caused by munitions, including submunitions". China, while not known as a user of cluster munitions, produces, stockpiles and exports the weapons, and munitions of Chinese origin have been found in Iraq, Israel, Lebanon and Sudan.

The United States, while focusing its arguments primarily on the military effectiveness and need for cluster munitions, also reiterated their belief that existing laws were sufficient. As Borrie stated, "...the US insisted that a solution to the hazards to civilians that cluster munitions posed was simply a matter of more rigorous implementation of existing humanitarian law rules applicable to all weapons..."

Israel, another major producer, exporter, user and stockpiler of cluster munitions, was resistant to the idea of prohibiting or restricting the use of cluster munitions throughout the CCW and

Oslo processes. Israel justified its use of cluster munitions on Lebanon as falling within the purview of legally permissible action under international humanitarian law. Its primary objective during the CCW process was that non-state armed groups would not be permitted to acquire and use cluster munitions. They insisted that any discussion on the issue in the CCW framework should focus on prohibiting the transfer of these weapons to non-state armed groups. As a senior Israeli diplomat stated at a CCW conference: "The use of arms including submunitions by terrorists against Israeli citizens...raises serious questions regarding how such weapons reached those hands and how the international community can enhance its control over the transfer of those weapons to rogue groups...This...should be the focus of future actions under the CCW framework..." In general, while they stated that international law as it stood was sufficient, were any discussions on cluster munitions or ERW needed, Israel's position was that such discussions were best concluded under the aegis of the CCW.

Russia, a major producer, exporter and user of cluster munitions, declined to participate in the Oslo Process as it claimed that its input was not regarded. Russia has used cluster munitions extensively in Chechnya between 1994 - 1996, and in 1999, and it also used cluster bombs in 2008 in Georgia, although they denied doing so. In its statements at the CCW Group of Governmental Experts session, Russia not only expressed its opinion that existing international law was adequate but also argued that the problems associated with using cluster munitions were "mythical" and could be avoided with accurate targeting of the weapon to minimize civilian damage. Throughout the negotiations on cluster munitions within the CCW, Russia maintained the position that discussions on a "protocol" were premature, and should instead focus on a "proposal".

On occasion, a state that initially believed that a further international treaty regarding this matter was not necessary, eventually came around towards supporting it. In 2007, the Australian Department of Defense argued in front of the Senate that the existing rules concerning cluster munitions were sufficient, and no further regulation was needed. However, at the Dublin Diplomatic Conference in May 2008, Australia joined the other states in adopting the final convention text.

All Explosive Remnants Are Equal

The United States also opposed the ban on the grounds that NGOs were unnecessarily singling out cluster munitions, instead of giving the proper focus to the entire category of unexploded ordnance. The US Department of Defense (DoD) argued in a white paper: "The debate about cluster munitions should not distract the international community from the fact that tens of thousands of survivors from landmines and the full range of Explosive Remnants of War (ERW) have been physically, emotionally, and economically harmed over the years". In the white paper, the authors point to the lesser proportion of harm produced by cluster munitions as compared to other explosive remnants. According to them, "cluster munitions...represent a small percentage of the threat that unexploded remnants of war pose to civilian populations". They argue that in countries where cluster munitions are said to be a major problem, such as Afghanistan, Cambodia, Kosovo etc., the reality on the ground is that a small percentage of the issues concern cluster munitions, and the rest stem from far more pressing issues such as the security threat towards old, poorly maintained munition depots.

It was clear that the United States was not interested in participating in any form of regulation of the use of these weapons, and focused instead on addressing the problems of cluster munitions as an aspect of explosive remnants of war, through implementing existing humanitarian law and improving the reliability of the munitions. The Department of Defense stated that cluster bombs have similar failure rates to other weapons, such as gravity bombs, mortar rounds or artillery shells, although so far this is unproven. As stated earlier, even with a low failure rate, due to the sheer number of submunitions in every cluster bomb, "even a small initial failure rate can quickly translate into a major humanitarian problem". Additionally, many types of US cluster bombs have a higher than average failure rate, up to 30%.

The Department of Defense claimed that focusing on cluster munitions actually detracted from the real issue – which was the humanitarian effect of all unexploded ordnance. "The campaign to ban cluster munitions has endeavored to elevate a single type of munition to infamy rather than addressing the continuing need to clean up *all* explosive remnants of war, the vast majority of which are not cluster munitions". The DoD failed to mention, however, that the United States was one of the few developed nations that had failed to sign the anti-personnel mine ban treaty. Clearly, the US believes that neither landmines nor cluster munitions merits singling out for a ban, or pose a significant threat, despite around two-thirds of countries globally, and a large number of NATO members, realizing that the damage caused by these specific weapons outweigh the benefits to be gained from their use.

Focus Instead on Clearance

Rather than focusing on banning a specific category of munitions, the United States claimed that it was more productive to adopt an arms control approach, to regulate the technology and method of use and follow it up with humanitarian assistance and clearing of minefields post-battle. According to Assistant Secretary Mull, "the United States is deeply concerned about the humanitarian impact not only of just cluster munitions but really the whole range of munitions that are used in war. It's an absolute moral obligation to clean up…unexploded ordnance and weapons that are left lying around". The United States thus took the approach that cure was better than prevention in this instance. According to the US Department of Defense:

> To truly save lives, responsible governments and civil society should urge all states to take a comprehensive, humanitarian, impact-based approach to reduce the effect of landmines and all ERW and by providing more support to existing clearance and survivors' assistance efforts, and *not dissipate resources in a variety of competing and redundant mechanisms* (emphasis added).

The importance of clearance (removal of unexploded ordnances from an area by experts) cannot be underestimated in post-conflict rehabilitation. Clearance of fields and residential areas must be done for the safety of civilians, and this is costly, with the affected countries often not being able to afford to carry it out without the support of other states. The United States is one of those states that have provided support for clearance efforts in countries that have been affected by ERW. Mull stated: "the United States is proud of the role that we've played in cleaning up battlefields around the world. Since 1993, we have spent more than $1.2 billion on cleaning up war zones and former conflict zones to make sure that they're safe for civilians to go back and reinhabit".

However, the assistance that has been provided by donor countries, while invaluable, does not extend to a 100% clean-up, still leaving thousands of unexploded ordnance in the countries affected, causing harm to communities that are unable to develop their lands, pursue agriculture or simply attend daily activities without the threat of mines and munitions in their path. Additionally, it is not enough to simply clean up the effects of cluster munitions and other unexploded ordnance. Preventing such weapons from causing civilian casualties and wide-scale destruction in the first place, especially when the drawbacks outweigh the benefits of use, is most important from the perspective of countries affected.

Opposition to the Venue and Process

Even when states accepted that an agreement regulating cluster munitions was crucial, some states objected to the Oslo Process precisely because it was a parallel process outside the UN system. They argued that a treaty that failed to get the support of the major military powers would not be effective. The objections of various states fell under three categories: an objection to going outside the United Nations structure, desiring to stay within the CCW (Convention on Conventional Weapons) framework and preferring to depend on domestic legislation.

Outside the United Nations Framework

The Oslo Process was necessitated because negotiations on banning cluster munitions stalled at the discussions under the United Nations and CCW framework. Powerful states that wished to continue to use cluster munitions with impunity lobbied to block any fruitful discussion that could lead to consensus on the issue. Ironically, these same states (and some others) cited the extra-official nature of the parallel process as a reason for refraining from participating or otherwise granting their full support. Even states that did contribute, expressed disappointment that the negotiations were conducted outside the official capacity. Bahrain participated in the Wellington conference, where it stated that "it was 'regrettable' that a conference of such magnitude and importance was not being held 'under the auspices of the United Nations'".

After the adoption of the Convention on Cluster Munitions in 2008 in Dublin, the United States declared that it chose not to participate in the process because it did "not support a sweeping ban on cluster munitions" and stated that it did not view the new Convention as establishing a norm against the use of cluster munitions. The US was against not only the theoretical conception of a ban but also expressed "disagreements about the right venue and the right tactics to follow in trying to solve the problem". Rather than support the Oslo Process, it would prefer to keep the negotiations under the aegis of the Convention on Conventional Weapons, a venue that includes the major military powers and producers of the world. According to Assistant Secretary Mull:

> We're not trying to stop countries from going to Oslo or to threaten them with punishment if they go, and if a country decided unilaterally that it will not use cluster munitions, we... certainly respect that. That's up to - to every country to make its own decision. We decided not to go to Oslo because we don't want to give weight to a process that we think is ultimately flawed, because we don't think that any international effort is going to succeed unless you get the major producers and the users of these weapons at the table. And it was clear to us that the Oslo process was not going to bring those participants. So we don't want to start a process that, in the end, is not going to be very effective in reaching our own humanitarian goal of limiting the risk that these weapons can pose to innocent civilians.

It is difficult to see a consistency in approach in the various statements from the United States. On one hand, they claimed to be interested in "limiting the risk that these weapons can pose to innocent civilians"; while on the other hand, they refused to participate in a process that had the support of at least half of the world's countries, more than half of NATO, half the producers and at least half of the countries that had stockpiled cluster munitions. Despite the US's objections to participating in the Oslo Process, they were obviously not objecting to the need to protect civilians from the munitions. They were one of the first states to consider the humanitarian impact of the munitions: in Kosovo, the high number of civilian casualties from the US' use of cluster munitions caused President Clinton to suspend their use in that war.

It is thus possible that the United States' objections were primarily to the process by which the weapons were regulated, and not necessarily to the regulation of the weapons themselves. The US responded to Norway's announcement to initiate the Oslo Process by stating: "the US government was disappointed at the announcement...of a separate meeting to go outside this CCW framework to have talks and to negotiate concerning cluster munitions. While recognizing that this is an important humanitarian issue, the process to deal with cluster munitions, we feel, should be one that is inside the current framework, the framework of the CCW. The effort to go outside, we think, is not healthy for the CCW, is not healthy for the development of widely adhered to rules of international humanitarian law...."

Perhaps, the concern of the United States was not the "health of the CCW", but their inability to control the outcome (and preserve their vested interests) if the discussions were to be held outside the CCW forum. While not participating directly in the Oslo Process, the US tried to influence the negotiations by communicating its various concerns directly to states, and especially influencing the article on interoperability (joint military operations between non-signatories and parties to the Convention). Victims of cluster munition attacks and campaigners protested the United States' lack of support and simultaneous attempt to undermine the Dublin negotiations, calling it the "elephant not in the room" during the Oslo Process.

Participation in the CCW Process

Despite the failure of states to find agreement on the issue of cluster munitions through the CCW process, the parallel process received much criticism for veering away from the official UN framework. Some of those who objected initially ultimately became signatories to the Convention, but still continued to express their opinion that the CCW was a more inclusive venue. One such state is Australia, who stated: "We remain of the view, however, that the [CCW] is the most appropriate forum...particularly since it includes the major producers and users of cluster munitions who have chosen to stay outside the Oslo Process".

Argentina initially supported the proposal for an international agreement regarding cluster munitions, participating in the initial conference launching the Oslo Process and endorsing the Oslo Declaration. However, it stated its preference for concluding the agreement within the UN framework, and despite contributing positively to the process, for instance on broadening the definition of victims within the Convention, ultimately Argentina was not present at the signing conference.

The most vocal objection to going outside the CCW process came from the United States, as stated above, in all probability because they would then be unable to control the agenda and outcome. The US has stated several times that they prefer to restrict the discussion of cluster munitions to the CCW process - "we believe that that venue is the right place to solve this because it is the place where all of the principal producers and users of these munitions vote and participate and work together". However, during the discussions in CCW review meetings, the US has consistently raised objections or sought to dilute the provisions regarding cluster munition regulation.

The United States is a party to the Convention on Conventional Weapons (CCW) and ratified Protocol V on Explosive Remnants of War on 21 January 2009. Protocol V was negotiated between 2001 - 2003, during which the United States refused to discuss or agree to any provisions relating to restrictions on the use of any specific categories of weapons such as cluster munitions, and only agreed to provisions on post-strike clearance of ordnance. This likely reiterates their inherent objections to any restriction on a weapon that the US already possesses in large numbers, as well as finds convenient to use, in contrast to their claim that they are simply opposed to the venue of the regulation. Additionally, it is likely that the US finally ratified Protocol V in 2009 due to perceived international pressure and stigma at the altered status of cluster munitions after the adoption of the Convention.

In 2006, after the excessive use by Israel of cluster munitions in its war with Lebanon, States Parties to the CCW increased calls for a separate legally-binding international instrument on cluster munitions; however, the United States was one of the states that objected to the introduction of new legislation, and they instead emphasized implementing existing legislation governing this issue. The US stance on the issue of cluster munitions underwent a transformation in the months leading up to the next CCW meeting in June 2007, when they were willing to debate the issue of cluster munitions, as long as it remained within the CCW Process. Steve Goose, co-chairman of the CMC, argued that this was more an attempt to stave off the Oslo Process rather than a genuine interest in negotiating an agreement regarding cluster munitions.

By November 2008, the United States was strongly supporting a draft protocol on cluster munitions within the CCW process. The US favored an optional set of restrictions on cluster munitions, which would mean in practice the replacement of 95% of the cluster munitions in its stockpiles. It also insisted on the necessity of a transition period, opposed a deadline for stockpile destruction, and proposed weakening language on victim assistance taken from the Convention on Cluster Munitions. While the US supported provisions for assistance to the victims of cluster munitions, it was among the few states that objected to including a broad definition of victim to encompass the victim's family and affected communities, one of the ground-breaking provisions adopted by the Convention on Cluster Munitions. It was evident that its own self-interest in lobbying for watered-down provisions, and the nature of the CCW venue, which gave the US relative political power to achieve its aims, was the primary driver of their interest in remaining within the CCW process for discussions on cluster munitions.

Domestic Legislation

Even the United States Congress appeared to not be the correct venue to debate this issue, as the Senate Amendment 4882 to the FY 2007 Defense Appropriations Bill (H.R. 5631) proposed in September 2006, was defeated 30 - 70. This piece of legislation was spearheaded by Senator Dianne Feinstein and co-sponsored by Senator Patrick Leahy, and sought to prevent the use of cluster munitions in or near civilian populations, to "protect civilian lives from unexploded cluster munitions". The amendment also sought to limit the export of these weapons only to countries that pledged to likewise not use them in or near civilian populations.

The following year, in February 2007, during the 110th Congress, Senators Leahy and Feinstein (with Representative James McGovern), introduced the "Cluster Munitions Civilian Protection Act of 2007", an act that would limit use and transfer of cluster munitions to those with a 99% minimum reliability rate, and limit their use in or near civilian areas. It would also require clean-up of submunitions mandated by the United States President if cluster munitions were used by the US or a country that received its supplies from the US. Although this act gathered support in the Senate and House of Representatives, it was not brought to a vote. Interestingly, in the briefing with Ambassador Mull in 2008, his primary objection to the ban on cluster munitions, aside from the inappropriateness of the venue, was the fact that cluster munitions, although potentially less useful in counter-insurgency measures, would be critically useful in a more traditional warfare setting, to counter the advance of enemy troops. If that were true, there ought to be no objections to passing a law prohibiting the use of the weapons near civilians, as these weapons are least efficacious when used in urban or dual-use environments.

Despite the lack of concrete progress in banning cluster munitions or restricting their use, the legislators in the US recognized that the submunitions failure rate was a problem. In December 2007 Congress passed an act that placed a one-year moratorium on the transfer of cluster munitions unless they have a 99% or higher tested reliability rate. The legislation also required that any state receiving cluster munitions from the US must agree that those cluster munitions will only be used against clearly defined military targets and will not be used in areas where civilians are known to be present.

Exceptions and Delays

Even states who were in favour of banning cluster munitions wanted exceptions and delays in implementation to benefit themselves. At the Vienna Conference, a group of states describing themselves as the "Like-minded group", formed to discuss changes to the draft treaty. Among these states were Australia, Canada, Czech Republic, Denmark, Finland, France, Germany, Italy, Japan, the Netherlands, Slovakia, Sweden, Switzerland, and the UK. At the Wellington Conference, they submitted proposals calling for exemptions and exclusions to the definition of cluster munitions, transitions and a provision on interoperability. These proposals were criticized by many as weakening the draft agreement.

Exceptions and Exemptions

Many states called for exemptions in the agreement for certain types of munitions. The Like-minded group had a common set of concerns regarding the agreement, including lobbying for the ability to retain so-called "good" cluster munitions. They argued vociferously to include exemptions for certain "more reliable" cluster munitions, notably those in their own arsenals. There were various perspectives put forward, with some states calling for exclusions for weapons that were not deemed to function like cluster munitions, and others wanting to exclude from the ban weapons that did function as cluster munitions, but weren't as "bad", had lower failure rates or were seen to be technologically more advanced. At the Wellington conference, the demands for proposals that included these concerns, along with the need for a transitional period for states to develop or acquire alternative weapons, dominated many of the discussions and led to significant conflict among the states.

A user, producer and stockpiler of cluster munitions, although part of the Oslo Process, the United Kingdom was initially among the countries that wanted exceptions to the categories of cluster munitions banned for weapons in their own arsenal. Among the exemptions proposed were "direct fire" munitions and those with less than a certain number of submunitions. However, the UK later changed its policy, ratifying the Convention and destroying its stockpiles of the weapon well before the deadline. Canada was another supporter of the proposals requesting exceptions to the definition. Additionally, Germany proposed at the Wellington Conference that states should be allowed to retain some cluster munitions for training and research purposes, and this proposal was supported by many of the Like-minded group.

Some states believed that there were different levels of cluster munitions, and they should be dealt with in differing ways. The Netherlands proposed a three-tier system of prohibition, with the worst offenders banned outright, the middle-range of weapons subject to certain restrictions, and complete exemptions for a limited few types of munitions. Slovakia, among other states, proposed exemptions for cluster munitions with self-destruct or self-deactivation mechanisms and those with a failure rate of less than 1%. However, at the Vienna Conference, the Norwegian Defense Research Establishment released a report analyzing the failure rates of munitions used by Israel in 2006, many of which failed despite having self-destruct mechanisms, and this report effectively undercuts the arguments for exemptions based on lower failure rates or self-destruct mechanisms.

Transition Period

Some states also proposed a transition period, giving states time before they needed to implement the provisions of the treaty. France, while a supporter of the Oslo Process, was one of the states that pushed for a transition period before the effect of the prohibition. It also made a statement at the end of the Wellington Conference, stating its dissatisfaction that not all views were properly considered.

Many other states that have not ratified the Convention cited a transition period (in some cases a lengthy one) as necessary, among them Russia, Slovakia, Turkey, South Korea and Israel. During the CCW protocol discussions, India supported a flexible transition period, allowing each state to decide for itself when the protocol would enter into force.

Regulation of Use Rather Than Ban

India, a producer, stockpiler and importer of cluster munitions, is a party to the Convention on Conventional Weapons (CCW) as well as its Protocol V. While India was "prepared to negotiate an instrument…that strikes a balance between military and humanitarian concerns", it was willing at best to accept regulation of its cluster munitions use, and not prohibition. Additionally, India was not willing to accept a deadline for destruction of stockpiles (in fact, it was not willing to destroy its stockpiles till they expired). Early in the Oslo Process, Sweden was another state that was not willing to adopt the prohibition and advocated for regulation of the use of certain munitions and not an outright ban. Switzerland had a similar stance, but both states adopted the treaty.

Interoperability

One of the most controversial issues during the negotiations for the cluster munition ban, was the issue of *interoperability*, or the legality of joint operations between countries that were part of the treaty and those that were not. The United States argued that banning cluster munitions would make it illegal for them to provide aid on peacekeeping missions as their ships contain cluster munitions as part of their weapon arsenal. As Stephen D. Mull, Acting Assistant Secretary of State for Political-Military Affairs stated at a briefing in Washington, an unintended consequence of the Convention would be to jeopardize the ability of the US to operate in alliance with signatories of the treaty. Despite their refusal to participate in the Oslo Process, the United States lobbied behind the scenes for exceptions to the Convention to allow such missions and other operations with States Parties.

Other states also professed doubts regarding the issue of joint operations. Australia shared concerns over interoperability at the Wellington conference. It introduced a discussion paper which argued that the prohibition on assistance as contained in the Wellington draft text "could inhibit a range of military activities essential to the effectiveness of international operations", which was supported by several other members of the Like-minded group. At the Dublin conference in May 2008, Australia continued to argue for the inclusion of provisions on interoperability, calling it essential to the agreement, and something that could not be addressed through national statements, but needed amendments to the Convention text. However, at the inclusion of the interoperability clause, Australia joined the consensus regarding the treaty and adopted the Convention.

The draft text of the Convention was amended, and Article 21 of the Convention on Cluster Munitions thus allows States Parties to engage in military activities with non-parties to the Convention. Although some campaigners believe that this article waters down the text of the treaty, this provision effectively nullified a major objection of many states to the cluster munition treaty.

Despite the varied and vigorous objections by many states to both the content and the method of the negotiations surrounding the cluster munitions ban, the Oslo Process succeeded. The next chapter highlights some of the main factors that contributed to the process of reaching consensus on the issue.

5

STRATEGY, INSIGHT AND TIMING
FACTORS THAT AIDED THE BAN PROCESS

Rarely if ever in international diplomacy have we seen such single-minded determination to conclude a convention with such high humanitarian goals in such a concentrated period of time.
- Mr. Micheál Martin, Irish Minister, Dublin Conference Closing Ceremony

DESPITE DECADES OF STALLING ON A CLUSTER MUNITION BAN, AND roadblocks faced by a process that was seen by some states as lacking legitimacy and proper authority, the Oslo Process and accomplished its aim of a comprehensive and binding agreement on the use of cluster munitions within the stated deadline of December 2008. What factors explain the overwhelming support for the ban despite the long-standing presence of these weapons in many states' arsenals? How did some states go from completely opposing such a ban to adopting it and destroying their national stockpiles? How did an issue that failed to gain traction for years garner support from NATO members, allies of the United States, erstwhile producers of the weapon, as well as several nations from the developing world, many of whom were not even signatories of the Convention on Conventional Weapons and had not participated in discussions on explosive remnants of war before the Oslo process? This chapter attempts to answer these questions and looks at the primary factors that enabled this accomplishment.

Increased Global Attention to Cluster Munition Use

The beginning of the war on terror in 2001 coincided with an increase in the global debate on the effects of cluster bombs. Since the Kosovo campaign in 1999, cluster munitions have been used increasingly in larger numbers and with greater civilian casualties. This led to increased deliberation, both from civil society and within the military, of the ethics of using indiscriminate weapons that create such widespread humanitarian effects.

Escalating Use of Cluster Munitions Worldwide

The NATO campaign in Yugoslavia in 1999 was under intense global scrutiny as an avowed humanitarian intervention, and as a result, any loss of civilian life attributed to NATO forces were deemed unacceptable. Thus, their use of cluster munitions, which in several cases missed their targets entirely, as well as caused unintended civilian casualties, was criticized globally by the media and civil society. According to reports by Human Rights Watch, there were 90 separate incidents involving civilians, with over 500 civilian casualties in total during the Kosovo campaign. Of these, approximately 90 - 150 civilian deaths were caused by cluster submunitions. President Clinton was finally compelled to order US forces to stop using cluster munitions in May 1999, due to the widespread media attention following the death of civilians in the village of Nis from a cluster bomb missing its target and killing civilians in the marketplace and clinic.

The use of cluster bombs in Afghanistan in October 2001

again caught the attention of the media, due to the large number of bombs employed over a short period of time. Over six months, the United States dropped about 1200 bombs with around 250,000 bomblets. There were high numbers of civilian casualties during the campaign primarily because the cluster bombs were used in dual-use areas, i.e. where both combatants and civilians live or work in close proximity, violating the rules of international humanitarian law, as well as due to the Taliban's documented tendency to use villagers as human shields. Their use also posed problems for the movement of US ground troops, leading many soldiers to recommend the suspension of these weapons. Although US officials refused to comment on specifics, it is believed that cluster bombs were used throughout the Afghanistan campaign, even when targeting Al-Qaeda hideouts in caves and near villages and civilian settlements. Media and NGO outcry against the use of these weapons focused on their inaccuracy, as well as the destruction wrought on an already under-developed and backward area.

These concerns were repeated in Iraq, where the US and UK forces dropped more cluster bombs in three weeks than they had in Afghanistan in six months. Although the US forces dropped fewer cluster bombs in populated areas to minimize civilian casualties, some munitions strayed onto civilian areas and hit neighborhoods and schools. The Coalition forces also used a combination of weapons with newer technology (better guidance systems with lower civilian casualties) and outdated models (which cause larger numbers of casualties). Using these older models near civilian areas causes the problems of cluster munitions to be compounded, as the higher failure rates of older types of cluster bombs produce even more unexploded ordnance, and thus higher numbers of fatalities.

It has been argued that 'dumb' weapons like cluster munitions, which have indiscriminate effects and leave behind hundreds of thousands of explosive remnants, have no further place in modern warfare. Increasingly, as the way warfare is conducted changes, with more campaigns conducted near civilian populated areas, and an increased need for counter-insurgency measures, using such weapons causes far greater casualties and increases the need for post-conflict clearance and developmental assistance. The humanitarian impact of cluster munition use far outweighs their military effectiveness. This was apparent in their last decade and a half of use, in the varying combat scenarios in Afghanistan and Iraq in 2001 and 2003. Even Acting Assistant Secretary of State for Political-Military Affairs Stephen Mull himself admitted, that cluster munitions were primarily useful in traditional combat circumstances, such as where an enemy troop was advancing and they had to be stopped, and there were no civilians in the vicinity. This is a scenario that is increasingly rare in modern warfare conditions, and yet, it is the primary effectiveness of these dangerous weapons. Although many powerful militaries continued to stockpile and use cluster munitions, they privately recognized that the usefulness of these weapons was waning with the changing technology and environment of warfare in the twenty-first century.

The Lebanon Conflict

Although some states were already beginning to accept that cluster munitions caused excessive harm, the immediate need to prohibit their use was less apparent, and many states continued to instead vocalize the need for regulation and proper targeting. In the summer of 2006, Israel's repeated strikes against Lebanon, leaving behind a carpet of unexploded ordnance, incited the debate regarding their continued legal and ethical basis, providing an unintended fillip to the ban movement.

The strikes against Lebanon were the most extensive in any conflict since the 1991 Gulf War. The number of submunitions used in Lebanon was almost twice the number used in the Gulf

War, and almost fifteen times the number used by the US in Afghanistan. The munitions were used in a 1400 square kilometer radius, rendering all those living there effectively homeless until the area was successfully demined. Aside from the on-going civilian casualties, there was severe damage to crops and agriculture, adding economic stress to an already impoverished people. Civilians returning were killed or injured while attempting to rebuild their homes or till their fields, preventing them from rehabilitating the community. Clearance was a mammoth task, and international agencies were overwhelmed by its magnitude, unprepared and understaffed. By January 2008, 25 clearance personnel were injured and 17 killed by cluster submunitions.

Israel later claimed that they took all required precautions to ensure that they abided by the rules of international humanitarian law, and restricted themselves to legitimate military targets. They also argued that they were forced to target civilian areas to defend themselves from missiles launched from villages by Hezbollah. Human Rights Watch, an international NGO that conducted an in-depth investigation into the effects of cluster munition use in Lebanon in 2006, concluded from their survey of the strike areas and questioning of surviving civilians that Israel's claims lack a basis in fact, or at the very least, are very difficult to prove. It appears that only a small percentage of the strikes against villages involved military targets, and the blanket bombing near civilian settlements bordered on the intentional targeting of civilians. One such strike hit a hospital with over 375 civilians and military noncombatants, trapping them inside for hours, with unexploded duds blocking the exits. This strike occurred some fifteen hours before the ceasefire.

Any attack that fails to differentiate between combatant and civilian targets during armed hostilities constitutes a breach of international humanitarian law, as dictated by the 1949 Geneva Conventions, which are considered customary international law. The actions of the Israeli Defense Forces (IDF) appear to have violated these rules of combat, with hundreds of strikes on civilian areas. The very nature of cluster munitions, that they cast a wide footprint and leave a large number of unexploded remnants behind, cause them to be seen as indiscriminate when used in civilian areas. Additionally, since many of the munitions used by Israel date from the Vietnam-era (supplied by the United States), they were technologically backward and had extremely high failure rates (estimated by clearance experts to be between 25 - 30%), leaving behind significantly high numbers of unexploded ordnance. Although Israel did issue warnings to civilians in South Lebanon via flyers and radio broadcasts, warning them to leave the area, not only would those unable to leave (for financial or health reasons) be killed; the area would be uninhabitable for civilians until the duds were cleared, no small task with duds numbering in the hundreds of thousands, possibly extending up to a million submunitions by some estimations, over such a wide area.

However, Israel maintained that they had not violated international law in their conduct during this period. The Israeli Defense Forces (IDF) issued a statement on December 24, 2007, on the results of its second internal inquiry into the conduct of its forces; both inquiries absolved the IDF of any breach of law or wrongdoing in this matter. As this report has not been made public, it is not possible to judge the rigor with which their investigation was carried out. However, as their interpretation of the events and their legality according to international humanitarian law appears to be at odds with that of other states and independent experts, it is likely that the investigation was conducted on assumptions about international law and / or facts which were vastly different from that acquired by NGOs and independent experts.

The events in Lebanon underscored the various problems associated with the use of cluster munitions: their high failure rate, the impossibility of limiting damage strictly to military personnel, the use of cluster munitions by non-state actors (Hezbollah), the impact on development and return to normalcy after conflict from the hundreds of thousands of unexploded duds. The egregious example provided by Israel's excessive use of cluster munitions in 2006 galvanized public opinion against these weapons and provided the justification to go outside the UN and CCW forum for those states that were already in favor of such an instrument, while providing the propelling force for those states on the fence, or otherwise lacking sufficient political motivation to work around the system instead of continuing to rely on winning within it. The Lebanon conflict also motivated the United Nations and the ICRC, who had previously been more cautious in calling for regulation on cluster munition use so as not to alienate those governments opposed to such regulation, to become more forthright in their positions and openly back the more radical Oslo process. In a way, therefore, the conflict in Lebanon acted as the tipping point, the final straw that caused events to be set in motion.

National Bans: Indicative of Changing Policy

Recognizing the problems with cluster munition use, even before the adoption of the Convention, some countries began to institute national legislation and policy regarding their use and production. Not only did this spur on those states to subsequently support a global ban, it also indicated to other countries the changing ethical landscape regarding the use of such weapons. Although most signatory countries came around to the idea of an outright ban in the months leading up to the Dublin negotiations, the stage had been set, in some cases a few years in advance, by the changing national policies of many forward-thinking states.

Restricting Failure Rates

The United States, despite their vocal objections to the Convention and every effort to prevent its existence, was one of the first states to create a national policy regarding cluster munitions. In 2001, US Secretary of Defense William Cohen issued a policy memorandum stating that all cluster munitions produced from 2005 onwards by the United States must have a dud rate (failure rate for submunitions) of less than 1%. In 2004, Denmark announced a temporary ban on the use and procurement of munitions with greater than 1% dud rate. The next year, Poland announced a 2.5% dud rate threshold for procurement.

While these measures were a positive step forward, they only took into account failure rates that were achieved under laboratory conditions, not actual battle conditions. As stated earlier, failure rates could significantly increase depending on the height from which the munitions were dropped, as well as the soil conditions in the place of deployment. Nevertheless, these measures were the beginnings of change in national policy, as countries began to recognize the significant humanitarian impact of these particular weapons.

Regulation of Use and Destruction of Stockpiles

Other countries have issued moratoriums on the use of cluster munitions for specific periods. In 2006, Norway issued a national moratorium on its use till failure rates could be properly tested. In February 2007, Austria followed suit with their own moratorium. Austria was also one of the earliest supporters of the international ban effort and was one of the "Core Group" countries. Hungary, the Netherlands and Croatia all announced national moratoriums on the use of cluster munitions in 2007. The following year, in 2008, Bosnia and Herzegovina, Bulgaria and Spain announced unilateral moratoriums on their use as well.

Some states also started to regulate stockpiles and begin to destroy the oldest and most defective models of munitions; these included Canada, Germany, Denmark, the Netherlands, Norway and the United Kingdom.

Comprehensive National Bans

In February 2006, Belgium was the first country to legislate a complete national prohibition on cluster munitions, including a ban on use, production, transfer and stockpiling, with a three-year deadline set for the destruction of stockpiles. In December 2007, Austria became the second country with a comprehensive ban, also committing to destroying stockpiles within three years. On 2 December 2008, Ireland passed legislation that ratified the Convention on Cluster Munitions as well as banned cluster munitions nationally, instituting a fine of €1 million and imprisonment for up to 10 years for violations.

Legislation on Investments

Many states and civil society organizations believe that the prohibition on assistance in the Convention on Cluster Munitions also includes a prohibition on investments in cluster munitions. As of June 2016, ten states have passed legislation to regulate and prohibit various forms of investment in cluster munitions. These ten states are Belgium, Ireland, Italy, Liechtenstein, Luxembourg, the Netherlands, New Zealand, Samoa, Spain and Switzerland.

A law passed in 2007 made Belgium the first country to legislate investment in companies that produce cluster munitions as a crime. Ireland's 2008 implementation law for the Convention on Cluster Munitions followed suit, including a historic disinvestment clause. In 2008, Luxembourg passed a draft law preventing persons or companies from "knowingly" financing cluster munitions. In 2004, the Norwegian Ministry of Finance precluded cluster munitions producers from receiving investment under the

Norwegian Government Pension Fund's ethical guidelines. In 2007, Dutch television aired a documentary titled "The Cluster-bomb Feeling", which explored the investments of pension funds in cluster munitions producing companies. This documentary created sufficient awareness and public outcry, that subsequently several pension funds announced their decision to end such investments.

These unilateral national policies signaled the changing tide of state opinion, although initially confined to the European and Eastern European region. Many of these states provided support for the Oslo Process, and illustrated to states in other regions that the use of cluster munitions was no longer considered acceptable conduct.

Lessons Learned From Ottawa and the Mine Ban Campaign

Some of the success of the Oslo Process and the cluster munition campaign can be imputed to its learning lessons from the campaign to ban landmines, undertaken in the late 1990s, culminating in the 1997 Mine Ban Treaty (Convention on the Prohibition of the Use, Stockpiling, Production and Transfer of Anti-Personnel Mines and on their Destruction). As stated by the co-chairman of the Cluster Munition Coalition:

> The Convention [on Cluster Munitions] contains excellent provisions on victim assistance, which are ground-breaking and historic in their own right. It has very good provisions on clearance, transparency, and international cooperation and assistance, all of which are an improvement on the Mine Ban Treaty, taking advantage of *lessons learned* over the past decade (emphasis added).

In many respects the campaign to ban cluster munitions is similar to that waged against the use of landmines by the

International Campaign to Ban Landmines, (hereinafter the ICBL); and the success of the Convention on Cluster Munitions echoes that of the treaty to ban landmines. The mine ban campaign had certain distinct advantages: they were focusing on a single, easy to understand issue, the content of the message was emotional and it had been demonstrated that landmines were no longer essential militarily or economically. This section analyses the reasons for the success of the Ottawa Process, the lessons learned by the ICBL and how they were implemented in the cluster munition campaign.

Why the Ottawa Process Succeeded

The tremendous and unexpected success of the landmine ban in the face of opposition from major world powers as well as stalled negotiations in the CCW process prompted international relations scholars to study the campaign and attempt to explain the success of the Ottawa Process. Historically, the issue was framed as one of arms control, as anti-personnel mines were frequently found to violate the principles of international humanitarian law (the law of armed conflict), and regulating or banning the weapons was initially approached from the perspective of regulating their use. However, as Steve Goose, one of the co-chairs of both the International Campaign to Ban Landmines and the Cluster Munition Coalition, stated: "Both as a reality of our work and as a political strategy, everyone agreed that we had to focus on the humanitarian side of things and not get hung up on arms control". Rather, the ICBL turned the discussion on anti-personnel mines into a *moral issue*; as an international relations scholar reiterated: "Invoking the norms of human rights had political as well as legal implications for a ban. Framing landmines as a moral issue turned the campaign *into a cause* (emphasis added)". It was this notion of a *cause* that propelled continuing interest and political action on this issue.

Although the Ottawa Process was a joint effort between concerned states, civil society and the United Nations, the ICBL played a significant role in its success. The role of NGOs in the Ottawa Process was three-fold - i) to highlight the shortcomings of the existing CCW process, ii) to call for a comprehensive ban on anti-personnel mines, and iii) to provide public awareness of the issue and undertake public relations. The ICBL especially excelled at this last task, continuing to keep the issue in the news, by releasing press statements and articles in news media throughout the process. According to a scholar, "the creative use of photography and other media in producing strong imagery helped to keep the human face of this issue before governments and was instrumental in the mobilization of publics". The issue was extremely conducive to garnering attention through images, both of the victims and of the progress of the campaign. For instance, the publicity for the landmine ban generated by Princess Diana's involvement was estimated to be equivalent to a $2 million public relations campaign. During the Ottawa Process, the predominant focus on the human face of the problem really paid off, paving the way for the later success of the cluster munition campaign by similar means.

The ICBL and other NGOs involved also complemented the multilateral negotiations and filled in gaps in the process. As one commentator noted, "the process that brought about the [land-mine ban] treaty itself has been heralded as a model for coopera-tion between governments and non-governmental organizations (NGOs)". The NGOs had several advantages that traditional international law-making processes lacked. The ICBL founding members had expertise, gained from extensive work with land-mine victims, that lobbyists and politicians lacked, which gave them credibility on the issue. They were able to focus exclusively on the issue and recognize problems and loopholes with the treaty faster and work to eliminate them. Their exclusive humani-tarian focus provided them with both credibility and a normative advantage. Most crucially, it appears that the NGO community themselves recognized their strengths, cataloging them in various publications discussing the landmine ban. According to one scholar, some of the factors which led to the success of NGO involvement in the landmine ban process were: i) a high resonance of goals between NGOs and the core group of states, ii) the existence of a patron government, iii) sufficient financing, iv) a media-friendly and morally unambiguous campaign issue, and v) the self-selecting nature of the process, with only states who accepted the Ottawa and Brussels Declarations allowed to participate. These conditions were repeated in the Oslo Process (only the patron government was different), which is certainly not a coincidence, and no doubt contributed to its success.

The campaign found that with coordinated action, they were able to achieve "rapid success" on what had earlier seemed an impossible goal. As international relations scholar, Leon Sigal noted, "making defense policy in Washington is an insiders' game, in which outsiders have not had much say over the past 50 years". Yet the campaign was able to demonstrate for the first time that success on an international agenda was possible outside the regular channels, and that small and medium countries, when they combined their efforts, could also achieve major diplomatic results.

Lessons Applied to the Oslo Process

The same factors that made landmines a pressing issue, brought to light the problems with cluster munitions. Landmines were seen to be exacerbating regional conflicts, rendering land useless to civilians, hindering post-conflict reconstruction and undermining infrastructure. Additionally, they violated the principles of international humanitarian law, as they mainly targeted civilians and caused "unnecessary suffering". Cluster munitions also caused the same problems, which had been highlighted at the same time as the land mine ban campaign, but the strong opposition by states to any form of regulation on cluster munitions had tabled the issue. When the campaign to ban cluster munitions gained momentum, it helped that states had already concluded a similar ban on anti-personnel mines.

There are many similarities between the contribution of the ICBL and that of the CMC. The similarities between the Oslo Process and the Ottawa Process suggest that the second time around, with the cluster munition ban, the stakeholders learned lessons from the land mine ban process which they simply applied to the cluster munition campaign. Both the ICBL and the CMC have many members in common, and in 2011, the two organizations merged to become the ICBL-CMC, working together to monitor the progress on banning both cluster munitions and landmines. Although the Cluster Munition Coalition (CMC) was a separate and unique entity from the ICBL at the time of the Oslo Process, the campaign shared some of the same organizations, and even the same individuals, and therefore attempted to repeat the success of the Ottawa Process. Hinting at this attempt, Steve Goose, co-chairman of the CMC, stated: "Can the phoenix rise from the ashes - again? Can lightning strike twice? Can the Oslo Process on cluster munitions replicate the Ottawa Process on antipersonnel mines?"

One of the similarities between the two processes was that they both grew out of the frustrations of the CCW Review process. In April 1996, a meeting was held of the "core group" countries who supported a landmine ban, many of which later supported the cluster munition ban as well. The Ottawa Process lasted 15 months, an accomplishment that probably gave credence to the similarly tight deadline established in the Oslo Conference. Both processes also focused on the humanitarian and moral aspect of the ban, instead of treating it as an arms control issue, which turned out to be an astute strategy.

It was clear that during the Ottawa Process, the ICBL stumbled onto a winning formula, and although each specific campaign and issue would have its own unique challenges, there were certain general best practices that contributed to the achievement of the ban. Steve Goose distilled the lessons learned from the mine ban campaign into recommendations for use in similar campaigns in the future. The ones that particularly resonate with the cluster munitions ban process are the recommendations for NGOs to focus not on arms control but instead on the human costs of the issues; provide expertise; "articulate goals clearly"; "speak with one voice"; "maintain a flexible structure"; include everyone and build in diversity from the beginning. These recommendations were clearly incorporated into the strategies of the cluster munition campaign and contributed to its success.

The role of NGOs in both processes could be seen as that of a 'connector', bringing the various actors together and driving the agenda behind-the-scenes. The NGOs brought to the table decades of expertise in working with victims, and in-depth knowledge of the provisions that needed to be included in the draft treaty. The NGOs used their knowledge to provide expertise to the negotiating states inside the process, while using their networks and experience with publicity to highlight the main aspects of the campaign in the media and public sphere, bringing attention to the ban campaign.

The mine ban campaign utilized the power of media and celebrity in putting a spotlight on their campaign. The issue lent itself well to the generation of powerful images, videos and articles; for instance, no one could forget the images of Princess Diana meeting with landmine victims and appealing for a stop to the use of these weapons. The efficacy of publicity efforts during the landmine campaign led the CMC to focus even more strongly on increased public relations efforts during Oslo; finding innovative ways to connect with the public, for instance driving the "Ban Bus" to engage the public during the Dublin Conference.

The nature of the ICBL, and its persuasiveness, contributed further to the campaign's success. The ICBL functioned not "as a coalition of 1000 organizations but rather as a single, homogenous bargaining voice with a unitary position". The ICBL spoke with a single voice and functioned as a single entity, which made it substantially easier to influence policy. Often even well-meaning advocates can fail to achieve anything due to disunity of method and message, a fate avoided successfully by both the ICBL, and its successor, the CMC.

How the Oslo Process Differed

Despite the similarities between the processes, there were some notable differences. The commencement of the Ottawa Process was almost accidental; although Canada was not initially a driving force, it later took on that role. Canadian Minister Lloyd Axworthy invited the assembled governments and NGOs to return to Ottawa in December 1997 for the treaty signing, an invitation that was unexpected and unpremeditated, unlike Norway's ownership of the Oslo Process from the first day.

Additionally, unlike in the case of landmines, there had been no special stigma attached to the use of cluster munitions, no special celebrity endorsements. Outside of those in the realms of policy and advocacy, most people had never even heard of cluster munitions or their drawbacks. Although the process of diplomacy that culminated in the achievement of the ban had its roots in the process used to achieve the landmine convention, the Oslo Process was more remarkable due to its success in banning a weapon that before the process started was seen as just another weapon in the military arsenal.

Another difference concerned the extent of participation of NGOs in the two campaigns. In the Ottawa Process, NGOs were involved from the start as they were the first to publicly call for a ban on anti-personnel mines; however, they were not automatically given a place at the table. The ICBL conducted a lot of behind-the-scenes lobbying at different stages to be allowed to send representatives to the various treaty discussion conferences, as well in the corridors outside the meetings to share critical information with the delegates negotiating the treaty. For instance, the ICBL informed pro-ban African delegates of the United States' effort to weaken the treaty, leading to galvanized support among those who opposed the proliferation of narrow self-interest from the major powers.

By the time the Oslo Process got started, the Cluster Munition Coalition was included far more readily, with opportunities given to delegates, especially victims from affected countries, to speak at the opening and closing ceremonies of the important conferences, as well as being allowed to present drafts and analysis to the governments for their consideration. The CMC also presumably learnt from the ICBL experience, as they too incorporated lobbying outside the meetings as an aspect of their strategy - to better leverage their expertise, and provide information to delegates strategically in order to lead to a stronger treaty outcome.

Accomplishing the goal of a ban on cluster munitions was far from a sure thing. Policy makers doubted whether the results of the ICBL could be repeated, viewing the success of the partnership between states and NGOs as "a one-off success". The atmosphere changed even more after the events of September 11, putting national security and defense firmly on the agendas of major governments as the top priority, making any humanitarian legislation even harder to find agreement on. Additionally, Canada received criticism for its role as the lead advocate on the mine ban issue, which might further have deterred other governments from volunteering for the same task. Nevertheless, Norway spearheaded the cluster munition campaign and the success of the ICBL in 1997 was repeated in 2008, 11 years to the day. As United Nations Secretary-General Ban Ki-Moon declared:

Exactly 11 years ago today, governments, international organizations, parliamentarians and civil society gathered for the historic signing of the Anti-Personnel Landmine Convention. That treaty...is a prime example of how a shared sense of conviction and determination can translate into concrete measures that save lives and livelihoods. In much the same way, the efforts of a broad-based coalition of States, international organizations and civil society has brought about this new Convention on Cluster Munitions, which further strengthens international humanitarian law. Not only will the convention prohibit the future use and proliferation of cluster weapons, it will also promote their very obsolescence.

Despite the difficult political and security climate, an even stronger treaty than the Mine Ban Convention was agreed upon and adopted, perhaps changing forever the rules of international diplomacy.

Nature of the Campaign

Another major factor in the success of the Oslo Process was the nature of the campaign itself, and the way it was conducted. Despite the objections to the process, and the formidable obstacles in its path, most notably from militarily powerful states who were adamantly against a complete ban on cluster munitions, the underdog campaign succeeded by employing some brilliant strategies and leaning into its inherent disadvantages.

Outside the UN System

Having the negotiations outside the UN system has helped the process to be efficient and fast.

– Firoz Alizada, International Campaign to Ban Landmines-
Cluster Munition Coalition

One of the reasons the Oslo Process succeeded was the venue of the process. Taking the negotiation outside the UN and the Convention on Conventional Weapons forum removed the need for consensus that caused the CCW process to stagnate in the first place. In seeking consensus, a few countries could block provisions that hurt their vested interests. It is clear in retrospect that legislation that faced strong opposition from even a small minority could never succeed through the CCW process, one of the primary reasons the protocol on cluster munitions being negotiated within the CCW has not yet found agreement. John Borrie stated in his book on the cluster munition process, *Unacceptable Harm*, that it was clear at a meeting convened by the International Committee of the Red Cross in 2000 on the issue of explosive remnants of war that "a weapon's alleged military utility would continue to trump humanitarian concerns about it in that setting [the CCW], no matter how serious those impacts were shown to be". Within the CCW venue, the need for using cluster munitions would always trump the need for ending such usage, especially since the system was predicated on the need for consensus.

The Oslo Process, by staying outside the UN system, was able to avoid these problems. As Steve Goose stated in his statement at the Dublin Conference in May 2008, "the fundamental basis of the Oslo Process has been that it is self-selecting: only those who choose to pursue urgently a prohibition on cluster munitions that cause unacceptable harm to civilians take part". The self-selecting nature of the process reduced the pressure to participate for states, making it voluntary rather than mandatory. Thus, states were able to *select into* the process, and the element of choice allowed many small and medium states to play an important part.

In addition, the independence of the venue provided a great boost to the process of getting agreement on a robust treaty. The CCW process, predicated on the need for consensus, was not conducive to the creation of a strong agreement, as some influential states strongly opposed any regulation of cluster munitions at all. The Oslo Process, on the other hand, followed different rules. They set a tight deadline for the conclusion of the process, as well as followed differing rules of procedure during the negotiation of the treaty text: where general agreement on an issue failed, the matter would be put to a vote. For substantive matters, decisions required a two-third majority, and for procedural matters, a simple majority. During the negotiations none of the issues needed to be brought to a vote, and although states could choose to opt out if they were not in agreement with the final text, all 107 states in attendance at the Dublin Conference adopted the Convention. The majority vote system allowed for comprehensive restrictions on use as well as far-reaching positive requirements that would not have been possible using a system of consensus. As Firoz Alizada from the ICBL-CMC stated: "Having the negotiations outside the UN system has helped the process to be efficient and fast".

Nature of the Message

Another primary reason for the success of the campaign was the nature of the message itself. The campaign to ban cluster munitions focused on one issue – the need to ban a weapon that was responsible for killing and injuring thousands of civilians, sometimes decades after the conflict was over. In their publicity and media messages, the campaign did not dilute the message, or make it overly complicated. In fact, I would argue that it was the opposite – the message was *sticky*.

In the book *The Tipping Point*, author Malcolm Gladwell made the point that one of the factors that determined the impact of a message, was its "stickiness". Gladwell defined this term as "the specific quality that a message needs to be successful...Is the message...memorable? Is it so memorable, in fact, that it can create change, that it can spur someone to action?" In my opinion, the message to ban cluster munitions succeeded because it was sticky, because it spurred governments and diplomats into taking action. The years of experience in advocacy and publicity for its various campaigns provided the cluster munition campaign with the ability to simplify the ban message to a few salient and attention-grabbing points. The message was clear – it is important to ban cluster munitions because they cause disproportional, unintended and unacceptable levels of harm to civilians, during and years after a violent conflict. The details were there for those who needed it, but the basic underlying message was not overly complicated by overwhelming amounts of data.

One of the reasons the campaign gained so much positive media attention and political interest was its emphasis on the human face of the problem, through images, films and telling the stories of the victims. As one ICBL-CMC campaigner expressed: "The campaign against cluster munitions successfully managed to convince the international community that banning cluster munitions is a matter of humanitarian concern, not security". Survivors attended the conferences during the Oslo Process, telling their stories and providing a real connection for delegates tasked with negotiating their countries' positions on the issue. It was difficult to ignore the pressing humanitarian nature of the problem and concentrate on military expediency when victims on crutches and wheelchairs spoke movingly of how one encounter with a cluster submunition upended and changed their entire life. At the Belgrade Conference of States Affected by Cluster Munitions, held in October 2007, the newly formed initiative of Ban Advocates (victims and survivors of cluster munitions attacks) spoke about the importance of a treaty banning the weapons. As stated by Borrie, "the Belgrade conference was especially important for the opportunity it gave to survivors of cluster munitions to make their voices heard".

Research on the effectiveness of leadership methods has shown that letting leaders initially outline their vision, while following up that vision with speakers who share personal stories is extremely effective in persuading listeners to take the action outlined or lend their support for the cause in question. As one of the co-authors of this research, Adam Grant, states, "...the most inspiring way to convey a vision is to outsource it to the people who are actually affected by it". Thus, involving cluster munitions survivors and sharing their stories to lend credence to the call by the CMC and the Core Group of countries to support the Oslo process was far more effective than the usual diplomatic process of speeches and lobbying by savvy insiders.

Multiple Avenues for Success

One of the reasons the success of the Convention is extraordinary is the change in the attitude of some states towards the ban. As stated in a Landmine Monitor report, "the period from 2006 until the end of 2008 saw *dramatic changes* in the positions of many governments on the military necessity and legality of cluster munitions. In a shift of international opinion, dozens of nations went from an adamant defense of the weapon to a full embrace of a comprehensive prohibition (emphasis added)". One of the reasons for this change is that during the Oslo Process, there were several chances to engage with the issues and for states to slowly change their thinking on this subject. Although it may have seemed "dramatic", it is likely that the multiple opportunities to engage the participants and discuss the issues that each conference provided, created the conditions for states to air out and resolve most of their concerns regarding banning a weapon that just months before, they had been reluctant to even contemplate giving up.

Part of the success of the Oslo Process (and the partnership) lay in its persistent and unique campaign. From one conference to another, starting from the Oslo conference in February 2007, to the final conference before negotiations in Dublin, in Wellington in February 2008 one year later, more and more countries participated or acted as observers to the process. At each conference, issues were discussed and parsed out, and although the draft provisions at times gained complexity, they also gained consensus.

The process started with the support of a few core countries, and slowly grew to include more than a 100 states. This was possible due to the repeated efforts at diplomacy on the part of the Cluster Munition Coalition and the Core Group at different global and regional summits, where they attempted to bring states on board on the issue. The conferences at Belgrade, Mexico City, Lima and Vienna helped to deliver the message of why the ban was urgently needed. The Cluster Munition Coalition and its partners also produced a remarkable amount of literature documenting the history of use of cluster munitions, the various humanitarian effects from using even the technical advanced models and the continued death toll attributable to them. All of this concerted expertise, presented over multiple avenues, contributed to persuading many more states to adopt the Convention.

Three-Pronged Partnership

One of the final factors that contributed to the success of the ban campaign was the successful partnership between states, civil society and the United Nations. Margaret Mead, the anthropologist said, "Never doubt that a small group of committed people can change the world; indeed, it is the only thing that ever has".

For social movements to succeed (and the campaign to ban cluster munitions can definitely be characterized as a social movement), a group of individuals or organizations must come together to work towards a 'single, unified goal'. The three-pronged partnership between states, civil society and international organizations flourished due to the unified front presented by the partners.

The partnership can be likened to a three-legged table; without one of the legs, the whole table would have toppled. Each of the partners brought something unique to the table. The Cluster Munition Coalition acted as the 'connector' – bringing together experts, victims, and states, as well as contributing publicity and first-hand knowledge of cluster munitions to the process. The United Nations provided funding and logistical support to enable smaller states and representatives, including survivors, from developing countries to participate; while the International Committee of the Red Cross (ICRC) contributed expertise, legitimacy and neutrality. The Core Group of states, who were committed to negotiating a binding agreement, helped to convince other states to join them, while taking the lead in diplomatic negotiations. In addition, the resources provided by Norway and other states helped the process to be inclusive of countries affected by cluster munition use and developing nations who would otherwise not be able to participate.

At various points during the Oslo process, civil society's contribution made the crucial difference to swaying the argument and discussion towards a more humanitarian and robust agreement. An influential report comprehensively detailing the impact of the use of cluster munitions around the world compiled by Handicap International influenced the agenda and the context of the Lima conference. At the Vienna conference, a report by Norwegian People's Aid showed conclusively that even those cluster munitions held up as technologically advanced and with significantly lower failure rates, in actual fact performed poorly in the field and proved fatal to both civilians and clearance personnel. The Cluster Munition Coalition and UNDP (along with other organizations) arranged for survivors to speak at the Belgrade conference (with funding from the Core Group states), which again for the participants, brought home the real humanitarian consequences of failing to reach an agreement on this tremendously important issue.

The three elements together accomplished what no one alone could. As stated by Thomas Nash at the signing conference at Oslo: "The success has come from so many invaluable individual contributions adding up to far more than the sum of the parts. It reminds us it is possible to change the status quo and we all have a responsibility to do it. It is simply wrong to justify inaction by saying it can't be done".

The various factors mentioned in this chapter – the increased global attention to the harm caused by cluster munitions, national bans on the use and production of cluster bombs by individual countries, lessons learnt from the success of the anti-personnel mine campaign and the successful three-pronged partnership between the stakeholders helped to build momentum for the campaign and achieve success within the limited timeframe agreed upon. The final text of the treaty is a testament to this process, in many ways standing out as a pioneering humanitarian agreement. The next chapter analyses the treaty provisions in further detail.

6

THE CONVENTION ON CLUSTER MUNITIONS

AN OVERVIEW AND ANALYSIS

The Convention on Cluster Munitions sets a gold standard for international weapons treaties.
– Human Rights Watch

AFTER YEARS OF STAGNATION AND DELAY, AFTER ROUNDS OF negotiation and intense lobbying, and decades of development setbacks from unexploded ordnance, the final text of the Convention on Cluster Munitions (hereinafter simply 'the Convention') rises above the fractured history of cluster munitions to provide an example of a strong and humanitarian international instrument. As expressed by Steve Goose, co-chairman of the Cluster Munition Coalition, during the Dublin Conference, "This can only be characterized as an extraordinary convention, one that is certain to save thousands and thousands of civilian lives for decades to come, and to provide both immediate and long-term relief and assistance to those already affected by the weapon". Not only did the convention text survive rounds of negotiation and remain true to its primary purpose, it was able to incorporate some ground-breaking provisions.

The overarching purpose of the treaty is set out in the Preamble itself. The Preamble to the Convention states the determination of the States Parties "to put an end for all time to the suffering and casualties caused by cluster munitions at the time of their use, when they fail to function as intended or when they are abandoned". While there are concerns about the language used in certain articles, an analysis of the text illustrates that this purpose has been largely achieved, at least in the intent and phrasing of the treaty. The strength of the Convention stems from its lack of exceptions: it bans *all* cluster munitions, from the time the treaty comes into force.

The Convention's twenty-three articles can be differentiated as containing negative obligations, which prohibit certain types of conduct, and positive obligations, which require a State Party to perform certain actions. This chapter provides an overview of the substantive articles of the Convention, as well as an analysis of its primary achievements and shortcomings.

Overview of the Convention

For the most part, the final text of the Convention on Cluster Munitions managed to avoid attempts to water down its language during the period of intense negotiations, creating a strong treaty that bans all types of cluster munitions without providing exceptions for individual states and particular technology. During the negotiations, there were attempts to allow exceptions for particular types of munitions owned by certain states, or munitions that might create less damage, or have a different sort of technology.

This was an echo of similar concerns raised during the negotiations for the landmine ban, but ultimately the States Parties agreed to ban all munitions that could be classified as a landmine.

As Goose stated in his statement to the signing conference in Norway:

> In the Mine Ban Treaty, which is hailed for its comprehensive prohibition on antipersonnel mines, the mantra has been, 'If it functions like an antipersonnel mine, it is an antipersonnel mine, and is banned.' The same is true of the Cluster Munition Convention. **If it functions like a cluster munition, it is a cluster munition, and is therefore banned.** If it has indiscriminate, wide-area effect and leaves behind large amounts of unexploded ordnance, it is banned (*emphasis added*).

Although the negotiations were tricky and protracted, the states participating in the drafting process for the Cluster Munition Convention eventually agreed that leaving room for exceptions for particular types of munitions would create a far weaker and less effective treaty. During this process, there was also a suggestion for including a transition period for implementation of the Convention, which was ultimately rejected. The Convention thus came into force once it achieved the agreed-upon threshold of 30 ratifications, on 1 August 2010.

The strength of this treaty lies in its comprehensive coverage of subjects concerning the use of cluster munitions. The Convention on Cluster Munitions not only prevents future use of the banned weapon, it also addresses the consequences of its past uses. Several articles of the treaty focus on post-conflict measures to reduce the aftereffects of the weapon's use. The text provides for clearance of cluster munition remnants within ten years of the treaty coming into force. Additionally, Article 4 of the Convention requires States Parties (states that have ratified the Convention) to assess the damage caused by cluster munitions within their jurisdictions and take steps to clear the areas, and also explicitly encourages user states to provide assistance to other members of the Convention who continue to be affected by the impact of unexploded remnants. The Convention explicitly applies to cluster munition use before its entry into force, and the text overall is designed to minimize the impact of the use of these weapons on civilians.

The first few articles of the treaty set out its purpose and scope, as well as define its applicability. Article 1 of the Convention states the general obligations of its States Parties:

> Each State Party undertakes never under any circumstances to: (a) use cluster munitions; (b) develop, produce, otherwise acquire, stockpile, retain or transfer to anyone, directly or indirectly, cluster munitions; (c) assist, encourage or induce anyone to engage in any activity prohibited to a State Party under this Convention.

Article 1(b)'s reference to "anyone" precludes even corporations and non-state armed groups from producing or transferring cluster munitions to individuals or organizations in other States Parties. This comprehensive ban applies also to explosive bomblets that are released by an aircraft. While this is the only mention of this additional banned type, commentators on the Convention have argued that the other provisions of the treaty apply similarly to this type of weapon as well. However, this might prove to be a controversial viewpoint in practice.

Article 2 contains definitions of relevant terms. The Convention provides a technical, specific definition of cluster munitions: "a conventional munition that is designed to disperse or release explosive submunitions each weighing less than 20 kilograms, and includes those explosive submunitions".

This definition differentiates cluster munitions from weapons that do not have similar characteristics, most crucially containing a large number of submunitions, or creating indiscriminate area effects. While there are, therefore "exclusions", the Convention does not contain "exemptions", and applies to all types of munitions that function as cluster bombs. As Steve Goose stated at the Dublin Conference, "the weapons that are covered in the Article 2(C) exclusion cannot have the indiscriminate wide area effect and excessive unexploded ordnance effect of cluster munitions, and thus should not be considered cluster munitions." The Convention also defines and includes within its scope "cluster munition remnants", which include failed, abandoned, and unexploded munitions. It is interesting to note, however, that the first definition included in the treaty, is that of "cluster munition victims". Thus, even before defining the banned munition, the Convention discusses those affected by its use, firmly establishing the humanitarian nature of this treaty.

Article 3 deals with the storage and destruction of weapons that have been stockpiled by states that ratified the Convention. Article 3(2) requires all States Parties to destroy their stockpiles as soon as possible, but no later than eight years after the entry into force of the Convention for that State Party. States can, however, request an extension of the deadline, by submitting a request to the meeting of the States Parties.

Article 5 enumerates the obligations of States Parties with relation to victim assistance; Article 6 sets out the obligations relating to international cooperation and assistance between States Parties in implementing the Convention, and Article 21 sets out the measures concerning relations with States not a party to the Convention. Articles 8 and 10 provide steps to be taken in the case of disputes between States Parties.

Article 4, the first positive obligation of the treaty, requires States Parties to clear cluster munition remnants in areas under "their jurisdiction or control" as soon as possible, but no later than ten years after its entry into force. The Convention stipulates certain steps such as survey, assessment, development of a plan and the fencing of contaminated areas that are mandatory. States Parties are also obligated to conduct risk reduction education to ensure that civilians are aware of the risks posed by explosive remnants.

Article 7 sets out obligations on transparency measures, requiring States Parties to report on national implementation measures and report on their progress and problems with putting into practice the obligations of the Convention. As expressed by Human Rights Watch, transparency advances implementation because it helps to identify which States Parties may need assistance in meeting their obligations, and also in monitoring the progress of the implementation of the Convention. States Parties are also obligated to submit an initial report on these subjects within 180 days of entry into force of the treaty to the United Nations Secretary-General, who will pass it on to other States Parties, thus facilitating the exchange of information among states.

Article 9 of the Convention requires each State Party to takes steps to implement its obligations, mandating that they "take all appropriate legal, administrative and other measures to implement this Convention." This requirement includes implementing criminal measures where necessary.

Innovative and Ground-breaking Provisions: Achievements of the Convention

The ban affects cluster munitions as an entire category of weapons. There are no wide exceptions, no transition periods. Its broad stigmatizing effect will hopefully also persuade states not participating here today to forsake these weapons.
– Statement by Austria, Oslo Signing Conference

The Convention on Cluster Munitions "advances international law with innovative provisions", such as those on victim assistance, user state responsibility for clearance, international assistance and transparency. There are two crucial achievements of the Convention: (1) the ban affects cluster munitions as a whole category of weapons, by broadly stigmatizing all types of cluster munitions with no exceptions; and (2) the provisions of the Convention covering victim support "set new humanitarian standards", covering comprehensively both pre- and post-conflict situations.

No Exceptions

This treaty has been likened to the Mine Ban treaty, but in many ways, the text of the Cluster Munitions Convention is even stronger, and an improvement on the landmine treaty, because of its comprehensive coverage of cluster munitions. As Steve Goose stated: "it bans not just some cluster munitions, but *all cluster munitions* (emphasis added)." The Convention bans not only all cluster bombs in existence but also any that might be produced in the future. The fact that there are no exceptions for specific categories of cluster munitions is remarkable given that just prior to the Dublin Conference, many states, notably Denmark, France, Germany, Japan, the Netherlands, Sweden, Switzerland and the United Kingdom, were lobbying for exceptions to certain types of weapons (those in their respective arsenals), claiming that those specific types were less harmful, had lower failure rates or had superior self-destruct capabilities. However, during the negotiations at Dublin, the provision to ban all cluster munitions with no exceptions for any specific type was agreed upon and included.

The Convention bans not only the use, production, stockpiling and transfer of these weapons, but also assistance with these activities. Article 1(1)(c) prohibits states from assisting non-States Parties with acts banned by the Convention. This is a very strong provision, unqualified and covering a broad meaning of the term "assistance". Additionally, the treaty contains provisions for victim assistance, which are "ground-breaking and historic in their own right", as well as strong obligations for clearance and international cooperation in removing existing munitions on the ground.

The Convention also provides for no time delays and no transition period; thus, states are obligated to destroy all stockpiles within eight years and end all use of the weapons immediately. Additionally, for the first time in an arms control agreement, the Preamble to the Convention on Cluster Munitions makes a reference to armed non-state actors, and affirms their obligations to adhere to the same obligations as the state they belong to, i.e. to be forbidden from using cluster munitions.

Victim Assistance

Articles 2 and 5 of the Convention on Cluster Munitions relate to victim assistance, and these are some of the treaty's strongest provisions. Article 2(1) defines "cluster munition victims" as "all persons who have been killed or suffered physical or psychological injury, economic loss, social marginalisation or substantial impairment of the realisation of their rights caused by the use of cluster munitions. They include those persons directly impacted by cluster munitions *as well as their affected families and communities*" (emphasis added). The definition of cluster munitions victims precedes even the definition of a cluster munition in the treaty document. By putting the definition of victims first, the Convention emphasizes its humanitarian origin and nature. Additionally, by including the words "as well as their affected families and communities", the treaty incorporates a wider understanding of the meaning of who constitutes a victim.

The Convention goes on to enumerate the assistance that victims must be given. Article 5 states that States Parties are obligated to "provide age- and gender-sensitive assistance, including medical care, rehabilitation and psychological support, as well as provide for their social and economic inclusion". The Convention sets out specifics on how states should provide this assistance, including assessing victims' needs, developing national laws, plans, and budgets, mobilizing resources, not discriminating among aid recipients, consulting with cluster munition victims, designating a government focal point to coordinate implementation and following best practices.

These articles in the Convention on Cluster Munitions are the first time a weapons treaty has included a definition of victim as well as a separate article on victim assistance. The wording *obligates*, rather than recommending or making it voluntary, which is a strong responsibility for States Parties. According to Human Rights Watch, the reference in the article to "applicable international humanitarian and human rights law" ensures that states will also have to meet the standards set out in the Convention on the Rights of People with Disabilities.

The statement by Austria at the Oslo Signing Conference summed up the significance of these provisions:

> The provisions on victim assistance set new humanitarian standards: [t]hey cover conflict and post-conflict periods, combatants and noncombatants, physical and psychological injury, and addressing not only the individual's immediate harm but also wider aspects of social and economic deprivation to families and communities. These provisions are the heart and soul of our new Convention. They should become the new international standard for victim assistance and they can, if we insist on raising the bar for victim assistance higher in all relevant fora.

International Cooperation and Assistance

A further achievement of the Convention is the requirement posed by Article 6, mandating those States Parties who are able to, or are in a position to do so to "provide technical, material and financial assistance to States Parties affected by cluster munitions". Therefore, Article 6 increases the power of the Convention by calling for more assistance than previous treaties and committing States Parties to providing resources to achieve the goals of the treaty. Without this pragmatic approach, the humanitarian obligations of the international community towards the victims of cluster munitions could easily become an unfulfilled empty promise, such as is often seen when providing assistance to victims in the context of other humanitarian issues.

Article 6 also enables states that have ratified the Convention to get assistance from other States Parties for undertaking activities such as cluster munition clearance and victim assistance which they might be doing anyway. Thus, states affected by cluster munitions have an additional incentive to join the Convention, as by doing so, they could benefit from financial assistance in clearing exploded remnants and providing victim support to affected citizens from other States Parties.

Recruitment and Norm Promotion

A further innovative achievement of the Convention is its positive obligation for states to 'recruit' other nations to the terms of the treaty. Article 21 of the Convention requires States Parties to "promote the norms it establishes" and "discourage States not party to this Convention from using cluster munitions", while encouraging them "to ratify, accept, approve or accede to this Convention". Despite Article 21 being the most controversial in the Convention, it is also one of the most ground-breaking, because the requirements to encourage other states to join and discourage them from violating the norms of the Convention appear in a weapons treaty for the first time.

. . .

Failures in Agreement: Criticisms and Weaknesses of the Convention

Despite the achievements and progressive articles of the Convention on Cluster Munitions, there are also some provisions in the text of the treaty that have been seen as taking away from the otherwise trailblazing nature of the agreement.

Interoperability

Article 21 in particular, which deals with joint military operations with non-States Parties, is seen by civil society and international law experts as undermining the Convention. For instance, Human Rights Watch in a formidable criticism of the article stated:

> ...Article 21 on interoperability is the *only stain on the fine fabric of the treaty text*. We are deeply disappointed with the language, which is not clear that foreign stockpiling and intentional assistance with prohibited acts are banned in all circumstances. We call on all states to clarify for the diplomatic record that Article 21 does not allow indefinite foreign stockpiling or intentional assistance. We will be watching very carefully to ensure that no state party engages in deliberate assistance with prohibited acts, or allows foreign stockpiling of cluster munitions on their territory in perpetuity, or undermines the fundamental obligations of the treaty in any way (emphasis added).

According to Steve Goose, co-chairman of the Cluster Munition Coalition, the text of Article 21 creates ambiguity regarding the provisions banning stockpiling and assistance with banned acts. The duties of States Parties during joint military operations are elucidated in paragraphs 3 and 4 of Article 21. Article 21(3) states in part that "States Parties, their military personnel or nationals, may engage in military cooperation and operations with States not party to this Convention that might engage in activities prohibited to a State Party". It allows members of the Convention to participate in operations with non-members, including crucially when the non-party state engages in activities that are banned under the Convention. Article 21(4) enumerates certain activities that remain prohibited in these situations and reiterates that States Parties themselves are not permitted to produce, stockpile, use or request to use cluster munitions under any conditions while engaging in joint military operations with non-States Parties.

These are among the most controversial provisions of the Convention. Military powers such as the United States, who declined to participate in the Oslo Process, sought to influence the text of the Convention and insert caveats for their own protection. The US was concerned that it would be unable to conduct joint military operations with its allies were they (the allies) to accede to the Convention, as the US military presumably would continue to possess cluster munition stockpiles. As Acting Assistant Secretary for Political-Military Affairs Stephen Mull stated at a briefing in Washington: "[the US is] concerned that measures adopted by the Oslo process could very much endanger [their] ability to operate and to cooperate with other militaries and other governments around the world...this would have very grave implications for a whole range of activities". Article 21 thus appears to appease countries such as the United States and other military powers who choose to stay outside the agreement, allowing States Parties to continue to conduct joint operations with countries that persist in using and stockpiling the banned weapon. This provision is understandably strongly denounced by civil society activists for undercutting the effect of the cluster munition ban.

. . .

Misinterpretation and Lack of Clarity

There are also some general instances of misinterpretation or lack of clarity in the text of the treaty. These include confirming whether the transit of cluster munitions is banned (separate from transfer of the weapons from one state to the other, which is prohibited); that investment, even indirectly, in the production of cluster munitions is prohibited; whether stockpiling is allowed on the territory of a State Party; and clarifying that all "intentional or knowing assistance with use of other prohibited acts is banned". As Steve Goose pointed out in his statement at the Signing Conference, it is important to get confirmation on these issues as quickly as possible, "so that state practice is consistent and in keeping with the letter and the spirit of the convention".

Some experts have additionally interpreted the wording of Article 21 to mean that the provisions of the Convention are nullified during joint operations, while other experts maintain that this article merely allows the participation of States Parties in such operations, without reducing the applicability of the treaty itself. Although arguably Article 21's clause on interoperability reduces the strength of the Convention as a whole, it is unlikely to have a negative humanitarian effect that is wide-reaching. It is inevitable that any international treaty that deals with weapons and matters of national security will have provisions that might be controversial; the interesting point to note is that the Convention on Cluster Munitions has only invited controversy regarding a single provision. This might further attest to the strength of the process by which the Convention came to life.

In conclusion, the provisions of the Convention on Cluster Munitions are ground-breaking, including for the first time in a weapons treaty, a definition of victims and mandatory provisions for victim assistance, as well as a total ban on the use of cluster munitions with no exceptions. However, the strength of the treaty will be judged on its implementation, as well as its contribution towards not only exerting compliance from the parties to the Convention but also its impact on global norms and attitudes regarding the usage of cluster munitions by *all* states.

7

AFFECTING LASTING CHANGE:
CREATING A NORM AGAINST THE USE OF CLUSTER MUNITIONS

This Convention on Cluster Munitions is a stunning example of how courageous, broad-based partnerships can face down even the most formidable challenges to human security and development. It is, however, the beginning of an exciting new phase in our battle against cluster munitions, not the end of the story.
– Kathleen Cravero, UNDP, Oslo Signing Conference

THE PRIMARY GOAL OF THE CONVENTION ON CLUSTER MUNITIONS, and those who worked towards accomplishing the agreement was to end the harm caused by cluster munitions. In order to put an end to the consequences of cluster munition use for good, it is essential not only for some states to pledge to uphold the provisions of the treaty, but for all states to stop producing, using or transferring cluster munitions, and destroy their existing stockpiles. Furthermore, just as in the case of anti-personnel mines, an international norm must be created, that prevents states from using the weapons because they are seen as prohibited under international law, binding even for states that have not ratified the

Convention.

An international agreement banning the use of cluster munitions can, therefore, be seen as the first step of a larger objective – establishing a norm against the use, production or transfer of cluster munitions globally. This is all the more crucial because unlike national laws, which are implemented and enforced by specific mechanisms, international law, having no enforcement mechanisms, relies on standards of behavior that states adopt and pledge to uphold.

As critics of the Convention on Cluster Munitions are quick to point out, it is far from universally accepted. Many states have not signed or ratified this Convention, including some states who were initially supportive of the Oslo Process. Many countries are still producing, stockpiling and transferring cluster munitions. In the six years since the signing of the Convention, while none of the countries who adopted the Convention on Cluster Munitions have violated its terms, several other states have used cluster munitions in violent conflicts. As the treaty stands currently, some of the major players in cluster munitions have remained outside the treaty process. What difference will that make to its implementation and success? In the future, will the United States, Russia or other military power that still stockpiles these weapons be deterred from using them?

Developing a norm against the use of these weapons is an ongoing challenge, and this chapter assesses the extent of the progress made in the past six years in implementing the Convention on Cluster Munitions, as well as its setbacks. Finally, it proposes a framework towards continuing this process and affecting lasting change in the quest to end the use of cluster munitions and their harmful effects on people globally.

Forming A Norm Against Usage

*The Convention is strong and ambitious...And even though we all know
there are important states not present, I am also convinced that together
we will have succeeded in stigmatising any future use of cluster
munitions.*
- Mr. Micheál Martin, Irish Minister, Dublin Conference Closing
Ceremony

Although changing norms of behavior can be difficult, adopting
the Convention begins the process towards altering the acceptable standard of conduct for states regarding the use of cluster
munitions. Experience with the Mine Ban Treaty showed that
even those who did not sign the treaty felt bound by the ban. As
Human Rights Watch stated: "Several of the world's biggest users
or stockpilers of cluster munitions were not present at the Dublin
talks, including the United States, Russia, China, India, Brazil,
Pakistan, and Israel. But experience with the Mine Ban Treaty
suggests that even non-signatories will ultimately feel bound by
the ban on cluster munitions. Although the United States has still
not signed the Mine Ban Treaty, for example, it has not used,
exported, or produced any antipersonnel landmines since the
treaty was negotiated..."

Those states that have not yet signed the Convention should
be encouraged to do so, especially erstwhile producer, stockpiler
and user states. Some of them, notably the United States, Russia,
China, India, Israel and Pakistan, are also major military powers,
and their remaining outside the Convention will reduce its effect
and the formation of a norm against the weapon. Coincidentally,
these states have also yet to accede to the Mine Ban Treaty.
Arguably, their lack of support may have less to do with the characteristics of the Convention on Cluster Munitions itself and
instead, reflects their reluctance to hinder their sovereignty on
military issues.

States Parties to the Convention are themselves the most crucial asset in bringing on board other states to acceding to the Convention. As Firoz Alizada, a campaigner with the ICBL – CMC stated: "Civil society organizations, and States Parties to the convention, work tirelessly to make the case towards states that are not yet on board the convention – explaining why they should join. In the meantime, the most crucial step for norm-building is for states to speak up when cluster munitions are used. They must publicly denounce and condemn such use as being inconsistent with the principles of International Humanitarian Law. This is already happening – over the past years, some 160 states have condemned the use of cluster munitions in Syria." As the number of countries that adopt the treaty on cluster munitions increases, the strength of their persuasion and their voices condemning on-going usage will gain more credibility.

For instance, the majority of the United States' allies as well as several NATO partners have signed the treaty, many of whom stockpiled and even used cluster munitions in the past; consequently, it might be politically difficult for the US to continue to use these weapons as part of its arsenal. The co-chairman of the Cluster Munition Coalition stated: "It is regrettable that the US and a handful of other states continue to insist on their need to use a weapon that the rest of world is banning because it causes unacceptable harm to civilians. But we believe that a strong new treaty will stigmatize cluster munitions to such a degree that it will be difficult for any country to use them without international condemnation."

The battle against the harmful effects of cluster munitions is far from won, but a few crucial victories have paved the way towards it. There are many encouraging signs of progress towards the formation of a norm regarding the use of cluster munitions. Some non-signatories have instituted temporary export moratoriums on cluster munitions transfers, while other states have established reliability standards for production. Twenty-seven states have destroyed their stockpiles of cluster munitions as of this writing (and many more states are on track towards doing so within their respective deadlines). The trend towards restricting financial investments in firms that produce cluster munitions is another important development. Each of these are important steps when seen individually, but taken together, they represent a shifting norm towards seeing cluster munitions as obsolete, dangerous weapons that should not, and do not, need to be used.

The Convention on Cluster Munitions remains the only international instrument on cluster munitions, after the Convention on Conventional Weapons (CCW) failed in 2011 to create a new protocol regulating these weapons. In order for the text of the treaty to be implemented, and not just remain a lofty aspiration, a sufficient number of states that previously used (or produced, transferred or stockpiled) cluster munitions must commit to stop using these weapons, halt production and destroy their stockpiles. As the discourse around this issue changes from usage and its humanitarian impact to that of clean-up, education and a mutual commitment to ending the effect of cluster munitions on civilian populations, the formation of a global norm against the use of such weapons will act as a deterrent against non-signatories to the Convention that might consider using cluster munitions in the future.

Progress in Implementation

The greatest success of the convention is that it works, it has started delivering from the first day.
– Firoz Alizada, International Campaign to Ban Landmines-Cluster Munition Coalition

Adoption of the Convention

The Convention on Cluster Munitions (CCM) entered into force on August 1, 2010. In order for the norm against the use of cluster munitions to strengthen, enough states must adopt the Convention on Cluster Munitions. Unfortunately, despite the initial support for the ban on cluster munitions, in the intervening years, there has been slow progress in adopting the Convention.

As of August 2016, 119 countries have joined the Convention, of which 100 are States Parties (i.e. they have ratified the Convention), and the remaining 19 are signatories who are yet to ratify the treaty. Of these, 42 states have or previously had stockpiles of cluster munitions, 16 were producer states, 7 states had previously used cluster munitions and 21 states had been affected by cluster munition use within its territory. Of those states that are not a party to the Convention, 49 currently has or previously had stockpiles of cluster munitions, 18 are producer states, 13 states had used cluster munitions before, and 19 are states in which cluster munitions have been used.

There has been slow adoption of the Convention in some regions, while it is faster in others. Forty-three of the 49 sub-Saharan African states have joined the Convention (28 States Parties and 14 signatories). Almost two-thirds of the European and American regions have signed or ratified the Convention (34 of 54 states in Europe and Central Asia, and 26 out of 35 states in the Americas). In stark contrast, only four states from the Middle East and North Africa (MENA) region are States Parties - Iraq, Tunisia, Lebanon and Palestine. Again, in the Asia and Pacific region, only a small handful of states have joined.

Part of the reason for slow adoption is that many of the states that have not yet adopted the treaty are small states with limited capacity for acceding. From the remainder, many states such as the United States, Brazil, Venezuela, Israel, India and Russia, have significant objections to the Convention. Many of these states are also those who objected to the Mine Ban Treaty. Additionally, 16 states adopted the Convention on Cluster Munitions in Dublin in 2008 but have yet to join. Fifty States Parties to the 1997 Mine Ban Treaty have also failed to join the Convention on Cluster Munitions.

In addition, there are states that have supported the Oslo Process, or at the very least, been active observers, but who have not yet joined the CCM. These states are not signatories to the Convention; however, they initially agreed with the need to stop the use, production and transfer of cluster munitions, and refrain from such use themselves. Cambodia, a supporter of the Oslo Process from the start, is one such state that has yet to sign the Convention. Egypt, a producer, importer and stockpiler, expressed support for the Oslo Process and attended the main conferences, endorsing the Oslo Declaration. However, it too has expressed reservations about the extent of the provisions, and declined so far to join.

Discontinuation of Production and Transfer

In the six years since the Convention was signed in Oslo, positive progress has been made on several fronts on ending the use of cluster munitions. The 17 former producer states that have joined the Convention have pledged to stop producing. Additionally, non-signatory Argentina has pledged to stop production and destroyed its stockpiles. At the same time, at least three of the currently producing countries (USA, Poland and South Korea) have established reliability standards for submunitions, with certain thresholds regarding their accepted failure rate.

In the past, 15 states transferred over 50 types of cluster munitions, to at least 60 other states. At present, 7 of those states are signatories to the CCM and have therefore committed to halting all transfers in the future. Non-signatories Singapore and the United States have also enacted export moratoriums.

. . .

Destruction of Stockpiles

The destruction of existing stockpiles of cluster munitions is crucial to progress towards the norm of the complete discontinuation of use of cluster munitions. According to the Cluster Munition Coalition, stockpile destruction has been one of the biggest successes of the Convention; many States Parties have already destroyed their stockpiles, and most others are on track to do so even before their treaty deadlines expire. The Cluster Munition Monitor estimates that before the ban campaign, 91 countries stockpiled millions of cluster munitions containing more than 1 billion submunitions. The number of countries who stockpile cluster munitions is now reduced from 91 to 47, and global stocks of cluster munitions have reduced significantly. As of August 2016, States Parties have already collectively destroyed nearly 1.4 million munitions and 172 million submunitions, representing 97% of States Parties' declared cluster munition stockpiles and 93% of total cluster munitions stockpiles.

Thirty-one countries that previously stockpiled cluster munitions have destroyed their stockpiles (29 are States Parties, of a total of 42 signatories and States Parties that stockpiled the weapon). The nations that have already completed destruction include the United Kingdom, Norway, the Netherlands, Belgium, Afghanistan, Japan, Canada, Germany, Iraq, Italy, Mozambique, France and Sweden. All other States Parties with cluster munitions stockpiles have committed to complete destruction within the eight-year deadline required by the Convention.

The number of cluster munitions reported as stockpiled by States Parties has increased significantly since previous reports, as initial Article 7 reports (requiring transparency from States Parties) have given more comprehensive data. Data regarding the stockpiles of states are hard to determine accurately, as they are based largely on analysis of publicly available information, which is dependent primarily on states' cooperation and their disseminating the relevant information. Additionally, most non-signatories to the Convention that stockpile cluster munitions have not disclosed detailed information on the quantities and types they hold. Therefore, it is not possible to make an accurate global estimate of quantities in stockpiles. However, despite the slight data discrepancies, the trend is that more and more states are destroying their stockpiles partially or completely. While the Convention allows States Parties to retain small numbers of munitions for training purposes, many states have further chosen to not retain any.

The statistics on current stockpiles of cluster munitions globally are rapidly changing as more States Parties are destroying their stockpiles. For instance, in the first edition of this book published in 2014, I reported that states had destroyed 68% of their munitions and 60% of their submunitions, with a total of 85 million submunitions destroyed. This number has now increased significantly, with a mere 7% of known cluster munitions stockpiles left in the possession of states. By the time you read this, in all likelihood, 100% of the stockpiles of States Parties would have been destroyed, a monumental step towards a cluster munition-free world.

Financial Disincentives

Another promising development in ensuring the success and universal acceptance of banning cluster munitions are the increasing number of disincentives enacted for investing in firms that produce cluster munitions. As of June 2016, according to PAX (Netherlands) in their global report on cluster munitions investments, 84 financial institutions worldwide have enacted such disincentives in some form or another.

Even before the adoption of the Convention on Cluster Munitions, some financial institutions terminated their investment in companies producing cluster munitions. According to the PAX report, 158 financial institutions worldwide still invest in companies producing cluster munitions, investing a total of US $28 billion (which has unfortunately increased by US$4 billion in the last few years).

However, there is a sign that some financial institutions are being proactive in changing their policies. IKV Pax identified 38 financial institutions that have enacted policies barring all investment in cluster munitions producers, while another 46 institutions have instituted mostly positive ban policies towards producers, with some notable exceptions. These 84 institutions taking the first step towards creating policies regarding cluster munitions investment illustrate the spreading of the norm against the use of these weapons. As IKV Pax Christi's report states: "the consensus among investors seems to be evolving. Where only a few financial institutions excluded companies producing cluster munitions when the Oslo process started, a wider group of investors seems to have become aware that producers of cluster munitions are not feasible business partners...[and] identifies investment in controversial weapons as a reputational risk". Some of the institutions with partial disinvestment policies include large financial conglomerates such as BNP Paribas, Barclays, HSBC and Royal Bank of Scotland.

Additionally, some states have adopted national legislation to ban investments in cluster munitions. As part of its ratification of the CCM, Italy adopted legislation that punishes "[w]hoever uses... develops, produces, acquires in any way, stores, retains, or transfers, directly and indirectly, cluster munitions or parts thereof, or financially assists, encourages or induces others to engage in such activity". More comprehensive draft legislation banning all Italian financial institutions from providing any form of support to producers of cluster munitions was introduced in 2010 and is likely that it will be adopted into law. Other countries that have adopted legislation banning investments include Liechtenstein, Luxembourg, Switzerland, Samoa, the Netherlands, Belgium (legislation adopted in 2006), New Zealand, Spain and

Ireland (the first country to include an investment ban along with the text ratifying the Convention).

All of these positive developments -- the discontinuation of production and transfer of cluster munitions, destruction of stockpiles and financial disinvestment regulations are all contributing to strengthening the norm against using cluster munitions and increasing the stigma of such use even by non-signatories. Unfortunately, it is feasible that a complete cessation of use and production is still a long way off, as demonstrated by the continued use of cluster munitions in the years since the treaty was negotiated.

Two Steps Back: Setbacks in the Norm Against Usage

There is no excuse for using cluster munitions that cause unacceptable harm to civilians; there is no middle ground between their use or non-use; there is no reason for allowing these weapons to continue killing and maiming days or even decades after a conflict has been settled or peace has been agreed.
- Ad Melkert, UN Under-Secretary General, Dublin Conference Opening Ceremony

Although there have been no confirmed reports or allegations of use of cluster munitions by any State Party or signatory since the Convention on Cluster Munitions was adopted in May 2008, there have been several instances of alleged or confirmed use of the banned weapons in the past few years. As stated by CMC campaigner Firoz Alizada, "a major challenge facing the convention is the ongoing use of cluster munitions. For example, cluster munitions are still being used in Yemen and Syria and some five non-signatories have used cluster bombs in 2014 - 2015. So the stigma is yet to be strengthened and universalized". While States Parties to the Convention have so far upheld the provisions of the treaty, use of cluster munitions by non-signatories undermines the creation of an international norm of eschewing these weapons completely.

Usage of Cluster Munitions Since 2008

The first use of cluster munitions after the start of the ban process was during the conflict between Russia and Georgia in South Ossetia in August 2008, where both sides allegedly used cluster munitions. Non-signatory Syria used cluster munitions extensively between 2012 and 2014, causing numerous civilian casualties. They were condemned by a significant number of states, including several non-signatories to the Convention. Both government and rebel forces have reportedly continued using the weapons since 2014 in the ongoing conflict in Syria. The government of Myanmar's forces may have also used a weapon prohibited by the Convention between 2012 - 2013. In 2011, government forces loyal to leader Muammar Gaddafi used cluster munitions in Libya in residential areas during its internal conflict. There is also credible evidence that cluster bombs were used in two locations in Libya in 2014.

In the border conflict in 2011, Thailand used cluster munitions in Cambodia over the Preah Vihear temple dispute. Although Thailand admitted to using weapons that could technically be described as cluster munitions, they denied the use of "cluster munitions", presumably not wanting to be associated with the rapidly stigmatized weapon. There have also been reports of cluster munition use in South Sudan in February 2014. UN Mine Action Service found cluster munition contamination near the town of Bor, on the road to the capital, Juba. It is not clear whether government or rebel forces were responsible for the use of the banned weapon. It is also alleged by Amnesty International that the United States used cluster munitions to attack a training camp in Yemen in 2009, although this was denied by the US.

Although the use of non-signatories to the Convention can be considered as detracting from the efficacy of the instrument, it has been argued by the Cluster Munition Coalition that the swift and widespread international condemnation by states, from both parties and non-parties to the Convention, illustrates the significant political cost to using these weapons and the "powerful stigma associated with the use of cluster munitions, a stigma that is now strong enough to dissuade most stockpilers from using or transferring the weapon, even those that are not part of the Convention".

Georgia

In August 2008, while the international community was in the process of banning cluster munitions, both Russia and Georgia used cluster munitions during their conflict over South Ossetia. The conflict took place less than three months after the Dublin Conference, where 107 states adopted the Convention on Cluster Munitions to ban the use of these weapons. The number of cluster munitions used was limited compared to recent conflicts in Lebanon and Iraq; however, the blatant disregard in using a weapon whose ban was being debated and rapidly reaching a consensus, shocked the international community and outraged activists who had been fighting assiduously for years against its use.

According to the Human Rights Watch report *A Dying Practice: Use of Cluster Munitions by Russia and Georgia in August 2008*, Russian forces fired cluster munitions into civilian populated areas of Georgia, in clear derogation of the principle of international humanitarian law requiring protection of non-combatants. The two parties to the conflict had widely varying histories with cluster munitions. Russia is a producer, exporter, stockpiler and prior user of cluster munitions (notably in Chechnya between 1994-1996, and again in 1999); while Georgia has never produced the weapons, or used them in the past, and imported the stock used in this conflict from Israel. The submunitions used by Georgia (of a type also used in Lebanon in 2006), are known for its high failure rates, which resulted in a high proportion of unexploded munitions.

Neither Russia nor Georgia were parties to the Convention; in fact, Russia had been consistently against the ban. However, the adoption of the treaty signaled a shift in international opinion regarding both the legality and morality of the use of cluster munitions, and according to Human Rights Watch, "their use of cluster munitions was in defiance of an emerging consensus on a basic prohibition". Russia and Georgia are also both bound by Protocol V to the Convention on Conventional Weapons, which they joined in 2008. While this protocol does not restrict the use of cluster munitions, it does include responsibilities regarding the protection of civilians.

Russia has repeatedly denied using cluster munitions during this conflict, despite mounting evidence to the contrary provided by international and local organizations. Georgia initially denounced the use of cluster munitions by Russia, then later acknowledged their own use, claiming, however, that they never targeted civilian areas. The Georgian Ministry of Defense claimed that they used the weapons exclusively against Russian military targets. However, when Georgian bought cluster munitions duds were found in villages near the border, they were forced to acknowledge the possibility of "an accident".

The high number of duds found inside the Georgian border, far away from any intended military targets, indicated that many of the weapons failed outright to hit the correct target. The duds also caused a humanitarian problem for their own people. Georgia continued to insist nevertheless, that their use of cluster munitions was successful, as they managed to "contain the

Russians for two days". This incident illustrates the dangers of this weapon - as they are seen to be useful even after they failed to deploy or hit the correct target, endangering their own citizens and leaving hundreds of duds within the borders of the country that used them.

Syria

From July 2012 till July 2016, human rights organizations have documented on-going and widespread use of cluster munitions with more than 360 cluster bomb attacks in a few hundred locations across Syria. The use of cluster munitions by the Syrian authorities have been condemned by more than 160 countries, however, cluster munitions (mostly Russian made) continue to be used in attacks across the country. Human Rights Watch has reported that Russian forces, in their joint operations with the Syrian authorities since September 2015, have used cluster munitions in several locations.

In July 2012, Syrian government forces commenced air strikes from helicopters against cities, towns, and neighborhoods under the control of opposition forces. Starting in October of the same year, cluster bomb strikes by helicopter became more frequent. The number of fatalities from cluster munition attacks number in the thousands. The Syrian Network for Human Rights states that more than 70 percent of the sites targeted are civilian areas and 97 percent of the victims are civilians, mostly children. According to Human Rights Watch, cluster munitions have been used repeatedly in Syria since 2014 by both Syrian authorities and the rebel forces. Most of these munitions have a high failure rate, resulting in large amounts of unexploded ordnance.

Implementing a Strategy of Gradation

In order for the use of cluster munitions to come to a halt, all states must ultimately join the Convention on Cluster Munitions.
– Firoz Alizada, International Campaign to Ban Landmines-
Cluster Munition Coalition

As argued in the introduction to this chapter, it is crucial that an international norm is formed against the continued use of this weapon in any form. This is even more important as certain states persist in producing, stockpiling and (a small minority), in using the banned munitions. It is essential for the strength of the ban that as many states join the Convention as possible, whether or not they have used, produced or stockpiled the weapon. With every new country that joins the Convention on Cluster Munitions, the global norm rejecting this weapon is strengthened and the protection for civilians becomes greater. "The most important thing this treaty does is to stigmatize cluster munitions," said Steve Goose, co-chairman of the CMC. "The stigma will grow and deepen over time, and ultimately make the use of cluster munitions unthinkable by anyone." The only recourse to containing and decreasing the impact of the continued use of cluster munitions globally is to strengthen the fledgling norm against its use.

In order for the norm against the use of cluster munitions to be strengthened, I believe that a two-pronged strategy must be pursued. Firstly, to encourage states that have not already signed onto the Convention to adopt it, and secondly, for states to implement intermediate steps that contribute towards reducing their engagement with cluster munitions.

Encouraging Increased Adoption

Engaging non-signatories to adopt the Convention is an ongoing, but difficult task. Of the 78 states that are not parties to the Convention, at least 30 have never produced, stockpiled or used cluster munitions. These states should be encouraged to join the Convention, as they have minimal obligations, and their joining the treaty further strengthens the norm against their use.

At the same time, the vast majority of states outside the Convention on Cluster Munitions, including those who have produced and / or stockpiled the weapons, have never used cluster munitions. Nine of the 16 non-signatories known to produce cluster munitions have stated that they have never used cluster munitions (Brazil, China, Egypt, Greece, South Korea, Pakistan, Poland, Romania and Turkey) and four other producer states have most likely not used the munitions either. The obligations of states that have never used cluster munitions are moderate, and several former producer states have joined the treaty and stopped production as well as destroyed existing stockpiles, while others have instituted export moratoria or more stringent standards. It is, therefore, feasible for those states that have not previously used the weapon to agree to give up their right to use and produce them in the future, although somewhat difficult to achieve.

Unsurprisingly, getting states who have used cluster munitions to adopt the Convention is significantly harder. Of the 20 states that have used cluster munitions in the past, three are signatories to the Convention, four have ratified it and 13 have not engaged with the treaty in any form. Of the non-signatory states, three could be considered significant users and producers of cluster munitions: Israel, Russia, and the United States (i.e. that they continue to produce and stockpile cluster munitions, and have used them in the last decade).

Therefore, in order to strengthen the norm against using cluster munitions, those states who have never used, produced or stockpiled the weapon should be encouraged to adopt the Convention, and given all assistance possible to simplify the process of ratification. Additionally, states who have never previously used the weapon should be encouraged to stop production and destroy their stockpiles, especially since the efficacy of cluster munitions have steadily reduced as warfare gets increasingly conducted in urban settings where such munitions clearly violate international law, as well as endanger the lives of the users' own soldiers. This approach, if successful, would considerably strengthen the norm, and as more states eschew the use of cluster munitions, the stigma and political consequences of its usage will outweigh its benefits.

Intermediate Steps Towards Adoption

If some states find the complete disavowal of cluster munitions politically or practically untenable at this juncture, the second approach towards strengthening the norm is to encourage non-States Parties to implement intermediate policies that reduce the negative impact of cluster munitions. Many states, including non-signatories to the Convention, have adopted certain policies that although do not go so far as to completely prohibit their use or production of cluster munitions, contribute towards lessening their impact and increasing transparency regarding the issue. Implementing one or all of these actions can not only reduce the problems caused by cluster munitions, they can contribute towards forming a robust norm against their further use.

States can be encouraged to undertake one or more of the following actions:

- Provide full disclosure regarding their existing stockpiles of cluster munitions.
- Destroy stockpiles of cluster munitions; at the very least, destroy those with a failure rate of more than 5%.
- Enact legislation that makes it illegal to invest in companies that produce cluster munitions.

- If the state continues to produce cluster munitions – enact legislation prohibiting the production of munitions with a greater than 1% failure rate.
- Issue a moratorium on the export or transfer of cluster munitions to other states.
- Issue a moratorium on the export or transfer of cluster munitions to non-state armed groups.
- Enact legislation that prohibits the use of cluster munitions near civilians and urban areas.
- Support clean-up efforts – for instance, by disclosing usage statistics to clearance teams, and providing financial and other assistance.

Some of these measures have already been taken by non-signatory states; for instance, Singapore and United States have issued a moratorium on the export of cluster munitions. For many states, instituting these measures can act as a gateway towards eventually ratifying the Convention on Cluster Munitions.

Adopting these intermediate measures will also contribute towards strengthening the norm against the usage of cluster munitions, and provide a powerful signal to those states that continue to produce, stockpile and use these weapons that ethically and legally their usage must be stopped and the impact caused by them in conflict mitigated.

8

CONCLUSION

AN UNPARALLELED FEAT OF
INTERNATIONAL DIPLOMACY

*[T]his treaty reaffirms and builds on the standards set by the Mine Ban
Treaty and the Convention on the Rights of Persons with Disabilities
that we celebrate today. Nobody should have any doubt now that we can
reach concrete global solutions to problems that seem beyond us and that
if we are going to succeed we need states and civil society working
together, rejecting the easy ways out, refusing to accept what some say is
'realistic' and instead building a new reality that becomes accepted as the
norm.*
– Thomas Nash, Oslo Signing Conference

ON A COLD DECEMBER MORNING IN 2008, REPRESENTATIVES OF
nearly a hundred states as well as dozens of civil society members,
gathered in Oslo City Hall to witness the signing of a treaty that
marked a moment of triumph and signaled a ray of hope for
humanitarian ideals. The treaty would outlaw a weapon that had
been in use since the turn of the previous century, one that had
destroyed the livelihoods of people for decades after its use and
disproportionately targeted civilians, especially children. This

weapon had contributed to the sluggish development of impoverished countries in South-east Asia, been used in multiple conflicts
in Afghanistan, Iraq and Lebanon, and was the dumbest of
weapons in an era characterized by smart technology and
weaponry. Despite all this, militarily powerful states were
unwilling to give up their dependence on this weapon, and not
only did they continue to produce and stockpile them for their
own use, the global trade in the weapon was brisk, with leftovers
from conflicts four decades earlier turning up in wars on the
other side of the world.

The journey towards adopting the Convention on Cluster
Munitions was fraught with obstacles and roadblocks along the
way. Broad agreement on the issues was made difficult with the
vocal opposition of a few key players, who not only opposed the
ban themselves, they also lobbied and pressured their allies to
oppose the ban as well. Nevertheless, over the course of eighteen
months, an unprecedented change took place in the international
landscape, as cluster munitions went from being considered militarily essential to being stigmatized and singled out for prohibition by many of the same states that formerly produced,
stockpiled and used them. Thomas Nash, the coordinator of the
Cluster Munition Coalition, stated at the Signing Conference in
Oslo:

> The conclusion of this Convention indicates a significant and
> fundamental change in the position of many governments that,
> until recently, regarded cluster munitions as essential to their
> security policies and military doctrines. *The importance of this shift
> cannot be overemphasized.* A great number of governments present
> here today, some with considerable defense and peacekeeping
> responsibilities, have concluded that their policies were not in full
> concurrence with their international obligations and could
> jeopardize recovery and development efforts. They decided not
> only to embrace their responsibility for clearance and victim

assistance, but also to revise their military doctrines...Indeed, today's signing conference also offers hope that States can depart from other long-held positions in the light of new evidence and new understandings of their own interests. Many areas...are ripe for precisely this kind of change (emphasis added).

The Oslo Process not only achieved its purpose within the confines of its tight timeline, but it exceeded the hopes of the international community by producing a strong and in many ways pioneering treaty. The treaty achieved its aim as summed up by Cluster Munition Coalition campaigner Alizada: "to stop the use of these devastating weapons and to address the consequences of past use (through demining and assistance to survivors of cluster munition explosions)". The Convention on Cluster Munitions not only bans all weapons that function like a cluster munition, it pioneers the definition of a victim and victim assistance in the context of cluster munition use. Despite the abstention of militarily powerful states such as the United States, Russia and China, enough states have ratified the Convention and taken positive action against cluster munitions (for instance, destroying their entire stockpiles and enacting legislation to prevent investments in cluster munition producers), that the use of the weapon is considered unethical and immoral even by many non-signatories to the treaty. As stated by Alizada:

The convention is successfully establishing that cluster munitions are unacceptable weapons. The US Ambassador to the United Nations, Susan Rice, listed the use of cluster munitions as an 'atrocity' of the Syrian regime. A spokesperson for the Russian Ministry of Foreign Affairs said cluster munitions were 'barbaric'. The Cluster Munition Coalition will continue to work relentlessly until the stigma against the weapons holds so strong that no armed forces dare to use them. This objective is also shared by all States Parties to the convention...

General Observations and Implications for the Future

*Nobody should have any doubt now that we can reach concrete global
solutions to problems that seem beyond us ...*
– Thomas Nash, Oslo Signing Conference

It is arguable that the unique approach to the adoption of the
Convention on Cluster Munitions provides a model for successfully addressing other equally pressing issues of humanitarian and
environmental concern. The success of the campaign to ban
cluster munitions illustrates that despite the Darwinian nature of
international diplomacy, where a few powerful states tend to
dictate the direction of global policy, individuals, civil society and
small and medium states have the power to shape international
law. While concerns about national security and sovereignty are
still uppermost in international negotiations, the campaign has
successfully illustrated that under the right circumstances, change
for good is still possible.

While each issue and situation is different, it is possible to
make certain general observations about the campaign that could
be repeated to address other humanitarian concerns:

1. **Focus on the Human Angle** – Whatever the issues are,
   there is always a human angle to the problem, and
   human victims that need to be protected. The campaign
   should highlight the real human cost of the issue, rather
   than simply relying on dry facts and figures. In the case
   of the cluster munition campaign, the focus was
   directed to the victims of cluster bombs and their

humanitarian cost, and survivors acting as spokespersons for the cause helped to highlight their plight.

2. **Keep the Issues Simple** – By keeping the issues and points of discussion simple, there is less room for ambiguity. The campaign focused less on complex military jargon and more on the few facts that conveyed the essence of the problem. They directed the attention of the public to the emotional aspects of the problem, making it easier for officials to lobby their own governments, as well as for the public to identify with the cause. For example, when I was writing this book, I could easily explain to friends and colleagues, in one or two sentences, the main reasons for undertaking the ban.

3. **Partnership with Civil Society** – The role of NGOs and civil society in the adoption of this treaty should not be underestimated, as they played a pivotal role in accomplishing the ban. They had a comparative advantage from their years of experience in working with victims' groups, as well as an in-depth knowledge of the issues. The members of the Cluster Munition Coalition published material that cited the publications of its members, and built off each other's research. They presented a unified front, both in terms of the logistics of the campaign, and in the resource literature. This is an often over-looked, but crucially important, point. Most issues of humanitarian concern have active civil society groups that possess the expertise to guide the issue; but, they rarely present one unified message or speak with one voice.

4. **Empowering Small and Medium States** – Although often it appears that the most powerful states set the agenda for all important issues in the global order, the

Convention on Cluster Munitions became a reality due to the efforts of dozens of small and medium states, who hosted and participated in the various conferences leading up to the Dublin negotiations. It is possible that this feat can be repeated if small and medium states could be sufficiently empowered and united to drive forward change on other important humanitarian concerns.

Where the above factors are present, it is likely that global cooperation can be accomplished on difficult issues, whether within official channels, or like the cluster munition and land mine bans, by taking the negotiations to a more suitable venue. The encore success of the Cluster Munition Convention and the Mine Ban Treaty has demonstrated that 'back-door diplomacy' is a successful route to agreements on otherwise seemingly intractable global issues. Not every issue, however, is ripe for this process, and it is not practical or desirable to take every issue outside the United Nations or other official channels. Instead, this author suggests that the success of the cluster munition ban should be seen as encouragement that pressing humanitarian problems can be addressed, and sometimes within a relatively short span of time, even if their solutions appear unattainable at present.

The Cluster Munition Convention was remarkable for its outcomes and for its aspirations. At a time when international cooperation on humanitarian objectives often falters, a coalition of NGOs and state partners managed to acquire consensus to ban a weapon that is still actively used. A deliberate act of rebellion brought about change in the military policy of many nations that months before the ban were still actively advocating to continue to use the weapon in question. Although the continued use of cluster munitions by certain nations even after the prohibition arguably dampens the accomplishment of the Oslo Process, the promotion of a norm against the use of cluster munitions that started to form with the commencement of the ban process, grew stronger with the addition of each signatory to the ban. The media attention received by the use of cluster munitions in the last half-decade serves as further proof that these uses are seen as unlawful and immoral, even when perpetrated by non-signatories to the Convention on Cluster Munitions. The very fact that more than half the countries of the world, including a large number of erstwhile users of the weapon, believe that cluster munitions are legally and morally harmful enough to prohibit all further use, has created a strong presumption that *all* countries will be bound, at least morally, to take into consideration before any further use.

Finally, the statement by the Austrian delegate at Oslo sums up the predominant sentiment: "This is a day of satisfaction and of hope...for the world: satisfaction that humanitarian disarmament initiatives are still possible and hope that what is possible for one category of weapons may be possible for others". Whilst the significance of the adoption of the Convention on Cluster Munitions must not be overemphasized, especially as several strong military powers have yet to accede to it, every victory on the international plane is hard won and must be cherished. It may be too soon to tell whether the results of the Oslo Process can be successfully replicated, but it is possible to declare without reservation that this success inspires movement on the international plane for other causes that have reached a plateau, and will perhaps stand out as a milestone signposting the moment in international relations where ordinary individuals were finally able to turn the tide of Westphalian sovereignty and herald an era where the plight of its citizens are just as important to heads of state as statecraft and power play.

BIBLIOGRAPHY

Books

- Christine Gray. *International Law and the Use of Force*. 2nd ed. Oxford: Oxford University Press, 2004.
- John Borrie & V. Martin Randin (eds). *Disarmament as Humanitarian Action: From Perspective to Practice*. United Nations Institute for Disarmanent Research, 2006.
- John Borrie. *Unacceptable Harm: A History of How the Treaty to Ban Cluster Munitions Was Won*. Geneva, Switzerland: United Nations Institute for Disarmament Research, 2009.
- Leon Sigal. *Negotiating Minefields: The Landmines Ban in American Politics*. New York, Routledge, 2006.
- Rae McGrath. *Landmines and Unexploded Ordnance: A Resource Book*. London, Pluto Press, 2000.
- Richard Anthony Matthew, Bryan McDonald, and Ken Rutherford (eds). *Landmines and Human Security: International Politics and War's Hidden Legacy*. Albany, State University of New York Press, 2004.
- Rosy Cave, Anthea Lawson, and Andrew Sherriff.

Cluster Munitions in Albania and Lao PDR: The Humanitarian and Socio-Economic Impact. Geneva, Switzerland: United Nations Institute for Disarmament Research, 2006.

Articles and Book Chapters

- David Atwood. "Banning Landmines: Observations on the Role of Civil Society", *Peace Politics of Civil Society,* June 1998.
- Jessica Corsi, 'Recent Development: Towards Peace Through Legal Innovation: The Process And The Promise Of The 2008 Cluster Munitions Convention', 22 Harv. Hum. Rts. J. 145, 2009.
- Kenneth R. Rutherford. "Nongovernmental Organizations and The Landmine Ban" in (eds). Richard A. Matthew et. al., *Landmines and Human Security: International Politics and War's Hidden Legacy.* Albany: State University of New York Press, 2004.
- Nicola Short. "The Role of NGOs in the Ottawa Process to Ban Landmines", *International Negotiation* 4: 481–500, 1999.
- Rosy Cave. "Disarmament As Humanitarian Action? Comparing Negotiations On Anti-Personnel Mines And Explosive Remnants Of War", in (eds.) John Borrie & V. Martin Randin. *Disarmament as Humanitarian Action: From Perspective to Practice.* United Nations Institute for Disarmanent Research, 2006.
- Stephen D. Goose and Jody Williams. "The Campaign To Ban Antipersonnel Landmines: Potential Lessons", in Richard A. Matthew et al. (eds.) *Landmines and Human Security: International Politics and War's Hidden Legacy.* Albany: State University of New York Press, 2004.
- Stephen D. Goose. "Cluster Munitions in the

Crosshairs: In Pursuit of a Prohibition", in (eds.) Jody Williams, Stephen D. Goose, and Mary Wareham. *Banning Landmines: Disarmament, Citizen Diplomacy, and Human Security*. Lanham, MD: Rowman & Littlefield, 2008, 217-239.

- Steve Goose. "Cluster Munitions: Ban Them". *Arms Control Today*, January/February 2008.

Reports

- Cluster Munition Coalition. *Cluster Munition Monitor 2010*. Ottawa: Mines Action Canada, 2010.
- Cluster Munition Coalition. *Global Treaty Status Overview*. April 2014.
- Cluster Munition Coalition. "Why and How All States Should Join The Convention On Cluster Munitions." March 28, 2014.
- Cluster Munition Coalition. *Stigma: The Political Costs of Using Cluster Munitions*. April 2014.
- Handicap International. *Fatal Footprint: The Global Human Impact of Cluster Munitions*. Handicap International, 2006.
- Handicap International. *Circle of Impact: The Fatal Footprint of Cluster Munitions on People and Communities*. Handicap International, 2007.
- Human Rights Watch. *Civilian Deaths in the NATO Air Campaign*. New York: Human Rights Watch, 2000.
- Human Rights Watch. *Fatally Flawed: Cluster Bombs and Their Use by the United States in Afghanistan*. New York: Human Rights Watch, 2002.
- Human Rights Watch, *Off Target: The Conduct of the War and Civilian Casualties in Iraq*, New York: Human Rights Watch, 2003.
- Human Rights Watch. *A Dying Practice: Use of Cluster*

Munitions by Russia and Georgia in August 2008. New York: Human Rights Watch, 2008.

- Human Rights Watch. *Flooding South Lebanon: Israel's Use of Cluster Munitions in Lebanon in July and August 2006.* New York: Human Rights Watch, 2008.
- Human Rights Watch. *Staying True to the Ban on Cluster Munitions: Understanding the Prohibition on Assistance in the Convention on Cluster Munitions.* New York: Human Rights Watch, 2009.
- Human Rights Watch. *Meeting the Challenge: Protecting Civilians through the Convention on Cluster Munitions.* New York: Human Rights Watch, 2010.
- Human Rights Watch. *Death from the Skies: Deliberate and Indiscriminate Attacks on Civilians.* New York: Human Rights Watch, 2013.
- IKV Pax. *Worldwide Investments in Cluster Munitions: A Shared Responsibility.* The Netherlands: IKV Pax, 2016.
- International Campaign to Ban Landmines – Cluster Munition Coalition (ICBL - CMC), *Cluster Munition Monitor 2013*, Ottawa: Mines Action Canada, September 2013.
- International Campaign to Ban Landmines – Cluster Munition Coalition (ICBL - CMC), *Cluster Munition Monitor 2015*, Ottawa: Mines Action Canada, September 2015.
- International Campaign to Ban Landmines – Cluster Munition Coalition (ICBL - CMC), *Cluster Munition Monitor 2016*, Ottawa: Mines Action Canada, September 2016.
- Landmine Action. *Failure to Protect: A Case for the Prohibition of Cluster Munitions.* Landmine Action, 2006.
- Landmine Monitor. *Banning Cluster Munitions: Government Policy and Practice.* Mines Action Canada, 2009.

- Rae McGrath, *Cluster Bombs: The Military Effectiveness and Impact on Civilians of Cluster Munitions*, Landmine Action, 2000.
- Syria Network for Human Rights. *Victims of Cluster Munitions in Syria: Government Forces Show No Respect to International Law and Continue to Use Cluster Munitions.* Feb 2, 2014.

Briefing Papers

- Andrew Feickert. "Cluster Munitions: Background and Issues for Congress". CRS Report, January 28, 2009.
- Human Rights Watch. "Cluster Bombs In Afghanistan: A Human Rights Watch Backgrounder". October 2001.
- Human Rights Watch. "Worldwide Production and Export of Cluster Munitions: A Human Rights Watch Briefing Paper". April 7, 2005.
- Human Rights Watch. "Cluster Munitions and the Proportionality Test: Memorandum to Delegates of the Convention on Conventional Weapons". April 7, 2008.
- Human Rights Watch. "Twelve Facts and Fallacies about the Convention on Cluster Munitions", April 14, 2009.
- United States Department of Defense White Paper. "Arms Control and International Security: Putting the Impact of Cluster Munitions In Context with the Effects of All Explosive Remnants of War". February 15, 2008.
- Secretary of Defense William Cohen, "Memorandum for the Secretaries of the Military Departments, Subject: DOD Policy on Submunition Reliability (U)," 10 January 2001.

Statements

- Ban Ki Moon. Secretary General's Message to the Signing Conference of the Convention on Cluster Munitions. Oslo: December 3, 2008.
- Cluster Munition Coalition. Statement To the Opening Plenary of the Dublin Diplomatic Conference on Cluster Munitions. May 19, 2008.
- Jonas Støre. "Banning Cluster Munitions – Making It Happen in Oslo". Foreword to the Convention on Cluster Munitions Signing Conference. Oslo: December 2 - 3, 2008.
- Kathleen Cravero. Statement at Oslo Signing Conference of the Convention on Cluster Munitions. Oslo: December 2 - 4, 2008.
- Rt Hon David Miliband. Secretary Of State For Foreign And Commonwealth Affairs. Statement on Signing The Convention On Cluster Munitions. Oslo: December 3, 2008.
- Statement by Austria. Oslo Signing Conference of the Convention on Cluster Munitions. Oslo: December 2 - 4, 2008.
- Statement by Mr. Espen Barth-Eide, Norway Deputy Minister of Defence. Oslo Conference on Cluster Munitions. February 22 – 23, 2007.
- Statement by the International Committee of the Red Cross. Oslo Conference on Cluster Munitions. February 22, 2007.
- Statement by Mr. Peter Batchelor, Chief, Conflict Prevention and Recovery Team, Bureau for Crisis Prevention and Recovery, United Nations Development Programme. Oslo Conference on Cluster Munitions. February 22 - 23, 2007.
- Statement by Patricia Lewis, United Nations Institute for Disarmament Research. "Translating challenges into political action: Some observations from a research

perspective". Oslo Conference on Cluster Munitions.
February 22 - 23, 2007.

- Steve Goose. Cluster Munition Coalition Statement To
the Committee of the Whole on the Agreement to
Adopt the Cluster Munitions Convention Dublin
Diplomatic Conference on Cluster Munitions. May 28,
2008.
- Steve Goose. Statement to the Signing Conference of
the Convention on Cluster Munitions. Oslo: December
3, 2008.
- Thomas Nash. Convention on Cluster Munitions
Signing Conference. Opening Statement. Oslo:
December 3, 2008.
- United States Ambassador Stephen D. Hull. "US Cluster
Munitions Policy". States News Service. May 21, 2008.

APPENDIX 1 – ACRONYMS

CBU cluster bomb unit
CCM 2008 Convention on Cluster Munitions
CCW 1980 Convention on Conventional Weapons
CMC Cluster Munition Coalition
ERW explosive remnants of war
HI Handicap International
HRW Human Rights Watch
ICBL International Campaign to Ban Landmines
ICRC International Committee of the Red Cross
IHL International humanitarian law
NATONorth American Treaty Organization
NGO non-governmental organization
UN United Nations
UNDP United Nations Development Programme
UXO unexploded ordnance

APPENDIX 2 – GLOSSARY

(This section is compiled from the Cluster Munition Monitor 2013 and Land Mine Monitor 2013.)

Abandoned explosive ordnance - Explosive ordnance that has not been used during an armed conflict, that has been left behind or dumped by a party to an armed conflict, and which is no longer under its control. Abandoned explosive ordnance is included under the broader category of explosive remnants of war.

Antipersonnel mine - According to the Mine Ban Treaty, an antipersonnel mine "means a mine designed to be exploded by the presence, proximity or contact of a person and that will incapacitate, injure or kill one or more persons."

Antivehicle mine - According to the Mine Ban Treaty, an antivehicle mine is a mine designed "to be detonated by the presence, proximity or contact of a vehicle as opposed to a person."

Clearance - Tasks or actions to ensure the removal and/or the destruction of all mine and ERW hazards from a specified area to a specified depth.

Cluster munition – According to the Convention on Cluster Munitions a cluster munition is "A conventional munition that is designed to disperse or release explosive submunitions each weighing less than 20 kilograms, and includes those explosive submunitions." Cluster munitions consist of containers and submunitions. Launched from the ground or air, the containers open and disperse submunitions (bomblets) over a wide area. Submunitions are typically designed to pierce armor, kill personnel, or both.

Convention on Cluster Munitions (CCM) – An international convention adopted in May 2008 and opened for signature in December 2008, which entered into force 1 August 2010. The convention prohibits the use, production, stockpiling, and transfer of cluster munitions. It also requires stockpile destruction, clearance, and victim assistance.

Convention on Conventional Weapons (CCW) – The 1980 Convention on Prohibitions or Restrictions on the Use of Certain Conventional Weapons Which May Be Deemed to Be Excessively Injurious or to Have Indiscriminate Effects, commonly referred to as the Convention on Conventional Weapons (CCW), aims to place prohibitions or restrictions on the use of conventional weapons about which there is widespread concern. It includes Protocol V on Explosive Remnants of War.

Demining - The set of activities that lead to the removal of mine and ERW hazards, including survey, mapping, clearance, marking, and the handover of cleared land.

Explosive remnants of war (ERW) – Under Protocol V to the Convention on Conventional Weapons, explosive remnants of war are defined as unexploded ordnance and abandoned explosive ordnance. Mines are explicitly excluded from the definition.

Interoperability – In relation to Article 21 of the Convention on Cluster Munitions, interoperability refers to joint military operations with states not party to the convention that might engage in activities prohibited to a State Party.

Oslo Process – The diplomatic process undertaken from

2006–2008 that led to the negotiation, adoption, and signing of the 2008 Convention on Cluster Munitions.

Risk reduction - Those actions which lessen the probability and/or severity of physical injury to people, property, or the environment due to mines/ERW. Risk reduction can be achieved by physical measures such as clearance, fencing or marking, or through behavioral changes brought about by mine/ERW risk education.

Submunition – Any munition that, to perform its task, separates from a parent munition (cluster munition). When airdropped, submunitions are often called "bomblets." When ground-launched, they are sometimes called "grenades."

Unexploded submunitions or unexploded bomblets – Submunitions that have failed to explode as intended, becoming unexploded ordnance.

Unexploded ordnance (UXO) – Munitions that were designed to explode but for some reason failed to detonate; unexploded submunitions are known as "duds."

Victim – According to the Convention on Cluster Munitions, "all persons who have been killed or suffered physical or psychological injury, economic loss, social marginalization or substantial impairment of the realization of their rights caused by the use of cluster munitions. They include those persons directly impacted by cluster munitions as well as their affected families and communities."

Victim assistance - Victim assistance includes, but is not limited to, data collection and needs assessment, emergency and continuing medical care, physical rehabilitation, psychological support and social inclusion, economic inclusion, and laws and public policies to ensure the full and equal integration and participation of survivors, their families, and communities in society.

APPENDIX 3 – THE CONVENTION ON CLUSTER MUNITIONS

CCM/77

30 May 2008

DIPLOMATIC CONFERENCE FOR THE ADOPTION OF A CONVENTION ON CLUSTER MUNITIONS DUBLIN 19 – 30 MAY 2008

CONVENTION ON CLUSTER MUNITIONS

The States Parties to this Convention,

Deeply concerned that civilian populations and individual civilians continue to bear the brunt of armed conflict,

Determined to put an end for all time to the suffering and casualties caused by cluster munitions at the time of their use, when they fail to function as intended or when they are abandoned,

Concerned that cluster munition remnants kill or maim civilians, including women and children, obstruct economic and social development, including through the loss of livelihood, impede post-conflict rehabilitation and reconstruction, delay or prevent the return of refugees and internally displaced persons, can negatively impact on national and international peace-building and humanitarian assistance efforts, and have other severe consequences that can persist for many years after use,

Deeply concerned also at the dangers presented by the large national stockpiles of cluster munitions retained for operational use and determined to ensure their rapid destruction,

Believing it necessary to contribute effectively in an efficient, coordinated manner to resolving the challenge of removing cluster munition remnants located throughout the world, and to ensure their destruction,

Determined also to ensure the full realisation of the rights of all cluster munition victims and recognising their inherent dignity,

Resolved to do their utmost in providing assistance to cluster munition victims, including medical care, rehabilitation and psychological support, as well as providing for their social and economic inclusion,

Recognising the need to provide age- and gender-sensitive assistance to cluster munition victims and to address the special needs of vulnerable groups,

Bearing in mind the Convention on the Rights of Persons with Disabilities which, *inter alia*, requires that States Parties to that Convention undertake to ensure and promote the full realisation of all human rights and fundamental freedoms of all persons with disabilities without discrimination of any kind on the basis of disability,

Mindful of the need to coordinate adequately efforts undertaken in various fora to address the rights and needs of victims of various types of weapons, and resolved to avoid discrimination among victims of various types of weapons,

Reaffirming that in cases not covered by this Convention or by other international agreements, civilians and combatants remain under the protection and authority of the principles of international law, derived from established custom, from the principles of humanity and from the dictates of public conscience,

Resolved also that armed groups distinct from the armed forces of a State shall not, under any circumstances, be permitted to engage in any activity prohibited to a State Party to this Convention,

Welcoming the very broad international support for the international norm prohibiting anti-personnel mines, enshrined in the 1997 Convention on the Prohibition of the Use, Stockpiling, Production and Transfer of Anti-Personnel Mines and on Their Destruction,

Welcoming also the adoption of the Protocol on Explosive Remnants of War, annexed to the Convention on Prohibitions or Restrictions on the Use of Certain Conventional Weapons Which May be Deemed to be Excessively Injurious or to Have Indiscriminate Effects, and its entry into force on 12 November 2006, and wishing to enhance the protection of civilians from the effects of cluster munition remnants in post-conflict environments,

Bearing in mind also United Nations Security Council Resolution 1325 on women, peace and security and United Nations Security Council Resolution 1612 on children in armed conflict,

Welcoming further the steps taken nationally, regionally and globally in recent years aimed at prohibiting, restricting or suspending the use, stockpiling, production and transfer of cluster munitions,

Stressing the role of public conscience in furthering the principles of humanity as evidenced by the global call for an end to civilian suffering caused by cluster munitions and recognising the efforts to that end undertaken by the United Nations, the International Committee of the Red Cross, the Cluster Munition Coalition and numerous other non-governmental organisations around the world,

Reaffirming the Declaration of the Oslo Conference on Cluster Munitions, by which, *inter alia*, States recognised the grave consequences caused by the use of cluster munitions and committed themselves to conclude by 2008 a legally binding instrument that would prohibit the use, production, transfer and stockpiling of cluster munitions that cause unacceptable harm to civilians, and would establish a framework for cooperation and assistance that ensures adequate provision of care and rehabilitation for victims, clearance of contaminated areas, risk reduction education and destruction of stockpiles,

Emphasising the desirability of attracting the adherence of all States to this Convention, and *determined* to work strenuously towards the promotion of its universalisation and its full implementation,

Basing themselves on the principles and rules of international humanitarian law, in particular the principle that the right of parties to an armed conflict to choose methods or means of warfare is not unlimited, and the rules that the parties to a conflict shall at all times distinguish between the civilian population and combatants and between civilian objects and military objectives and accordingly direct their operations against military objectives only, that in the conduct of military operations constant care shall be taken to spare the civilian population, civilians and civilian objects and that the civilian population and individual civilians enjoy general protection against dangers arising from military operations,

HAVE AGREED as follows:

Article 1
General obligations and scope of application

1. Each State Party undertakes never under any circumstances to:

(a) Use cluster munitions;

(b) Develop, produce, otherwise acquire, stockpile, retain or transfer to anyone, directly or indirectly, cluster munitions;

(c) Assist, encourage or induce anyone to engage in any activity prohibited to a State Party under this Convention.

2. Paragraph 1 of this Article applies, *mutatis mutandis*, to explosive bomblets that are specifically designed to be dispersed or released from dispensers affixed to aircraft.

3. This Convention does not apply to mines.

Article 2

Definitions

For the purposes of this Convention:

1. **"Cluster munition victims"** means all persons who have been killed or suffered physical or psychological injury, economic loss, social marginalisation or substantial impairment of the realisation of their rights caused by the use of cluster munitions. They include those persons directly impacted by cluster munitions as well as their affected families and communities;

2. **"Cluster munition"** means a conventional munition that is designed to disperse or release explosive submunitions each weighing less than 20 kilograms, and includes those explosive submunitions. It does not mean the following:

(a) A munition or submunition designed to dispense flares, smoke, pyrotechnics or chaff; or a munition designed exclusively for an air defence role;

(b) A munition or submunition designed to produce electrical or electronic effects;

(c) A munition that, in order to avoid indiscriminate area effects and the risks posed by unexploded submunitions, has all of the following characteristics:

(i) Each munition contains fewer than ten explosive submunitions;

(ii) Each explosive submunition weighs more than four kilograms;

(iii) Each explosive submunition is designed to detect and engage a single target object;

(iv) Each explosive submunition is equipped with an electronic self-destruction mechanism;

(v) Each explosive submunition is equipped with an electronic self-deactivating feature;

3. "**Explosive submunition**" means a conventional munition that in order to perform its task is dispersed or released by a cluster munition and is designed to function by detonating an explosive charge prior to, on or after impact;

4. "**Failed cluster munition**" means a cluster munition that has been fired, dropped, launched, projected or otherwise delivered and which should have dispersed or released its explosive submunitions but failed to do so;

5. "**Unexploded submunition**" means an explosive submunition that has been dispersed or released by, or otherwise separated from, a cluster munition and has failed to explode as intended;

6. "**Abandoned cluster munitions**" means cluster munitions or explosive submunitions that have not been used and that have been left behind or dumped, and that are no longer under the control of the party that left them behind or dumped them. They may or may not have been prepared for use;

7. "**Cluster munition remnants**" means failed cluster munitions, abandoned cluster munitions, unexploded submunitions and unexploded bomblets;

8. "**Transfer**" involves, in addition to the physical movement of cluster munitions into or from national territory, the transfer of title to and control over cluster munitions, but does not involve the transfer of territory containing cluster munition remnants;

9. "**Self-destruction mechanism**" means an incorporated automatically-functioning mechanism which is in addition to the primary initiating mechanism of the munition and which secures the destruction of the munition into which it is incorporated;

10. "**Self-deactivating**" means automatically rendering a munition inoperable by means of the irreversible exhaustion of a

component, for example a battery, that is essential to the operation of the munition;

11. **"Cluster munition contaminated area"** means an area known or suspected to contain cluster munition remnants;

12. **"Mine"** means a munition designed to be placed under, on or near the ground or other surface area and to be exploded by the presence, proximity or contact of a person or a vehicle;

13. **"Explosive bomblet"** means a conventional munition, weighing less than 20 kilograms, which is not self-propelled and which, in order to perform its task, is dispersed or released by a dispenser, and is designed to function by detonating an explosive charge prior to, on or after impact;

14. **"Dispenser"** means a container that is designed to disperse or release explosive bomblets and which is affixed to an aircraft at the time of dispersal or release;

15. **"Unexploded bomblet"** means an explosive bomblet that has been dispersed, released or otherwise separated from a dispenser and has failed to explode as intended.

Article 3
Storage and stockpile destruction

1. Each State Party shall, in accordance with national regulations, separate all cluster munitions under its jurisdiction and control from munitions retained for operational use and mark them for the purpose of destruction.

2. Each State Party undertakes to destroy or ensure the destruction of all cluster munitions referred to in paragraph 1 of this Article as soon as possible but not later than eight years after the entry into force of this Convention for that State Party. Each State Party undertakes to ensure that destruction methods comply with applicable international standards for protecting public health and the environment.

3. If a State Party believes that it will be unable to destroy or

ensure the destruction of all cluster munitions referred to in paragraph 1 of this Article within eight years of entry into force of this Convention for that State Party it may submit a request to a Meeting of States Parties or a Review Conference for an extension of the deadline for completing the destruction of such cluster munitions by a period of up to four years. A State Party may, in exceptional circumstances, request additional extensions of up to four years. The requested extensions shall not exceed the number of years strictly necessary for that State Party to complete its obligations under paragraph 2 of this Article.

4. Each request for an extension shall set out:

(a) The duration of the proposed extension;

(b) A detailed explanation of the proposed extension, including the financial and technical means available to or required by the State Party for the destruction of all cluster munitions referred to in paragraph 1 of this Article and, where applicable, the exceptional circumstances justifying it;

(c) A plan for how and when stockpile destruction will be completed;

(d) The quantity and type of cluster munitions and explosive submunitions held at the entry into force of this Convention for that State Party and any additional cluster munitions or explosive submunitions discovered after such entry into force;

(e) The quantity and type of cluster munitions and explosive submunitions destroyed during the period referred to in paragraph 2 of this Article; and

(f) The quantity and type of cluster munitions and explosive submunitions remaining to be destroyed during the proposed extension and the annual destruction rate expected to be achieved.

5. The Meeting of States Parties or the Review Conference shall, taking into consideration the factors referred to in paragraph 4 of this Article, assess the request and decide by a majority of votes of

States Parties present and voting whether to grant the request for an extension. The States Parties may decide to grant a shorter extension than that requested and may propose benchmarks for the extension, as appropriate. A request for an extension shall be submitted a minimum of nine months prior to the Meeting of States Parties or the Review Conference at which it is to be considered.

6. Notwithstanding the provisions of Article 1 of this Convention, the retention or acquisition of a limited number of cluster munitions and explosive submunitions for the development of and training in cluster munition and explosive submunition detection, clearance or destruction techniques, or for the development of cluster munition counter-measures, is permitted. The amount of explosive submunitions retained or acquired shall not exceed the minimum number absolutely necessary for these purposes.

7. Notwithstanding the provisions of Article 1 of this Convention, the transfer of cluster munitions to another State Party for the purpose of destruction, as well as for the purposes described in paragraph 6 of this Article, is permitted.

8. States Parties retaining, acquiring or transferring cluster munitions or explosive submunitions for the purposes described in paragraphs 6 and 7 of this Article shall submit a detailed report on the planned and actual use of these cluster munitions and explosive submunitions and their type, quantity and lot numbers. If cluster munitions or explosive submunitions are transferred to another State Party for these purposes, the report shall include reference to the receiving party. Such a report shall be prepared for each year during which a State Party retained, acquired or transferred cluster munitions or explosive submunitions and shall be submitted to the Secretary-General of the United Nations no later than 30 April of the following year.

Article 4

*Clearance and destruction of cluster munition remnants and risk
reduction education*

1. Each State Party undertakes to clear and destroy, or ensure the
clearance and destruction of, cluster munition remnants located
in cluster munition contaminated areas under its jurisdiction or
control, as follows:

(a) Where cluster munition remnants are located in areas
under its jurisdiction or control at the date of entry into force of
this Convention

for that State Party, such clearance and destruction shall be
completed as soon as possible but not later than ten years from
that date;

(b) Where, after entry into force of this Convention for that
State Party, cluster munitions have become cluster munition
remnants located in areas under its jurisdiction or control, such
clearance and destruction must be completed as soon as possible
but not later than ten years after the end of the active hostilities
during which such cluster munitions became cluster munition
remnants; and

(c) Upon fulfilling either of its obligations set out in sub-para-
graphs (a) and (b) of this paragraph, that State Party shall make a
declaration of compliance to the next Meeting of States Parties.

2. In fulfilling its obligations under paragraph 1 of this Article,
each State Party shall take the following measures as soon as
possible, taking into consideration the provisions of Article 6 of
this Convention regarding international cooperation and
assistance:

(a) Survey, assess and record the threat posed by cluster munition remnants, making every effort to identify all cluster munition contaminated areas under its jurisdiction or control;

(b) Assess and prioritise needs in terms of marking, protection
of civilians, clearance and destruction, and take steps to mobilise
resources and develop a national plan to carry out these activities,

building, where appropriate, upon existing structures, experiences and methodologies;

(c) Take all feasible steps to ensure that all cluster munition contaminated areas under its jurisdiction or control are perimeter-marked, monitored and protected by fencing or other means to ensure the effective exclusion of civilians. Warning signs based on methods of marking readily recognisable by the affected community should be utilised in the marking of suspected hazardous areas. Signs and other hazardous area boundary markers should, as far as possible, be visible, legible, durable and resistant to environmental effects and should clearly identify which side of the marked boundary is considered to be within the cluster munition contaminated areas and which side is considered to be safe;

(d) Clear and destroy all cluster munition remnants located in areas under its jurisdiction or control; and

(e) Conduct risk reduction education to ensure awareness among civilians living in or around cluster munition contaminated areas of the risks posed by such remnants.

3. In conducting the activities referred to in paragraph 2 of this Article, each State Party shall take into account international standards, including the International Mine Action Standards (IMAS).

4. This paragraph shall apply in cases in which cluster munitions have been used or abandoned by one State Party prior to entry into force of this Convention for that State Party and have become cluster munition remnants that are located in areas under the jurisdiction or control of another State Party at the time of entry into force of this Convention for the latter.

(a) In such cases, upon entry into force of this Convention for both States Parties, the former State Party is strongly encouraged to provide, *inter alia*, technical, financial, material or human resources assistance to the latter State Party, either bilaterally or through a mutually agreed third party, including through the

United Nations system or other relevant organisations, to facilitate the marking, clearance and destruction of such cluster munition remnants.

(b) Such assistance shall include, where available, information on types and quantities of the cluster munitions used, precise locations of cluster munition strikes and areas in which cluster munition remnants are known to be located.

5. If a State Party believes that it will be unable to clear and destroy or ensure the clearance and destruction of all cluster munition remnants referred to in paragraph 1 of this Article within ten years of the entry into force of this Convention for that State Party, it may submit a request to a Meeting of States Parties or a Review Conference for an extension of the deadline for completing the clearance and destruction of such cluster munition remnants by a period of up to five years. The requested extension shall not exceed the number of years strictly necessary for that State Party to complete its obligations under paragraph 1 of this Article.

6. A request for an extension shall be submitted to a Meeting of States Parties or a Review Conference prior to the expiry of the time period referred to in paragraph 1 of this Article for that State Party. Each request shall be submitted a minimum of nine months prior to the Meeting of States Parties or Review Conference at which it is to be considered. Each request shall set out:

(a) The duration of the proposed extension;

(b) A detailed explanation of the reasons for the proposed extension, including the financial and technical means available to and required by the State Party for the clearance and destruction of all cluster munition remnants during the proposed extension;

(c) The preparation of future work and the status of work already conducted under national clearance and demining programmes during the initial ten year period referred to in paragraph 1 of this Article and any subsequent extensions;

(d) The total area containing cluster munition remnants at the time of entry into force of this Convention for that State Party and any additional areas containing cluster munition remnants discovered after such entry into force;

(e) The total area containing cluster munition remnants cleared since entry into force of this Convention;

(f) The total area containing cluster munition remnants remaining to be cleared during the proposed extension;

(g) The circumstances that have impeded the ability of the State Party to destroy all cluster munition remnants located in areas under its jurisdiction or control during the initial ten year period referred to in paragraph 1 of this Article, and those that may impede this ability during the proposed extension;

(h) The humanitarian, social, economic and environmental implications of the proposed extension; and

(i) Any other information relevant to the request for the proposed extension.

7. The Meeting of States Parties or the Review Conference shall, taking into consideration the factors referred to in paragraph 6 of this Article, including, *inter alia*, the quantities of cluster munition remnants reported, assess the request and decide by a majority of votes of States Parties present and voting whether to grant the request for an extension. The States Parties may decide to grant a shorter extension than that requested and may propose benchmarks for the extension, as appropriate.

8. Such an extension may be renewed by a period of up to five years upon the submission of a new request, in accordance with paragraphs 5, 6 and 7 of this Article. In requesting a further extension a State Party shall submit relevant additional information on what has been undertaken during the previous extension granted pursuant to this Article.

Article 5
Victim assistance

1. Each State Party with respect to cluster munition victims in areas under its jurisdiction or control shall, in accordance with applicable international humanitarian and human rights law, adequately provide age- and gender-sensitive assistance, including medical care, rehabilitation and psychological support, as well as provide for their social and economic inclusion. Each State Party shall make every effort to collect reliable relevant data with respect to cluster munition victims.

2. In fulfilling its obligations under paragraph 1 of this Article each State Party shall:

(a) Assess the needs of cluster munition victims;

(b) Develop, implement and enforce any necessary national laws and policies;

(c) Develop a national plan and budget, including timeframes to carry out these activities, with a view to incorporating them within the existing national disability, development and human rights frameworks and mechanisms, while respecting the specific role and contribution of relevant actors;

(d) Take steps to mobilise national and international resources;

(e) Not discriminate against or among cluster munition victims, or between cluster munition victims and those who have suffered injuries or disabilities from other causes; differences in treatment should be based only on medical, rehabilitative, psychological or socio-economic needs;

(f) Closely consult with and actively involve cluster munition victims and their representative organisations;

(g) Designate a focal point within the government for coordination of matters relating to the implementation of this Article; and

(h) Strive to incorporate relevant guidelines and good practices including in the areas of medical care, rehabilitation and psychological support, as well as social and economic inclusion.

Article 6

International cooperation and assistance

1. In fulfilling its obligations under this Convention each State Party has the right to seek and receive assistance.

2. Each State Party in a position to do so shall provide technical, material and financial assistance to States Parties affected by cluster munitions, aimed at the implementation of the obligations of this Convention. Such assistance may be provided, *inter alia*, through the United Nations system, international, regional or national organisations or institutions, non-governmental organisations or institutions, or on a bilateral basis.

3. Each State Party undertakes to facilitate and shall have the right to participate in the fullest possible exchange of equipment and scientific and technological information concerning the implementation of this Convention. The States Parties shall not impose undue restrictions on the provision and receipt of clearance and other such equipment and related technological information for humanitarian purposes.

4. In addition to any obligations it may have pursuant to paragraph 4 of Article 4 of this Convention, each State Party in a position to do so shall provide assistance for clearance and destruction of cluster munition remnants and information concerning various means and technologies related to clearance of cluster munitions, as well as lists of experts, expert agencies or national points of contact on clearance and destruction of cluster munition remnants and related activities.

5. Each State Party in a position to do so shall provide assistance for the destruction of stockpiled cluster munitions, and shall also provide assistance to identify, assess and prioritise needs and practical measures in terms of marking, risk reduction education, protection of civilians and clearance and destruction as provided in Article 4 of this Convention.

6. Where, after entry into force of this Convention, cluster munitions have become cluster munition remnants located in

areas under the jurisdiction or control of a State Party, each State Party in a position to do so shall urgently provide emergency assistance to the affected State Party.

7. Each State Party in a position to do so shall provide assistance for the implementation of the obligations referred to in Article 5 of this Convention to adequately provide age- and gender-sensitive assistance, including medical care, rehabilitation and psychological support, as well as provide for social and economic inclusion of cluster munition victims. Such assistance may be provided, *inter alia*, through the United Nations system, international, regional or national organisations or institutions, the International Committee of the Red Cross, national Red Cross and Red Crescent Societies and their International Federation, non-governmental organisations or on a bilateral basis.

8. Each State Party in a position to do so shall provide assistance to contribute to the economic and social recovery needed as a result of cluster munition use in affected States Parties.

9. Each State Party in a position to do so may contribute to relevant trust funds in order to facilitate the provision of assistance under this Article.

10. Each State Party that seeks and receives assistance shall take all appropriate measures in order to facilitate the timely and effective implementation of this Convention, including facilitation of the entry and exit of personnel, materiel and equipment, in a manner consistent with national laws and regulations, taking into consideration international best practices.

11. Each State Party may, with the purpose of developing a national action plan, request the United Nations system, regional organisations, other States Parties or other competent intergovernmental or non-governmental institutions to assist its authorities to determine, *inter alia*:

(a) The nature and extent of cluster munition remnants located in areas under its jurisdiction or control;

(b) The financial, technological and human resources required for the implementation of the plan;

(c) The time estimated as necessary to clear and destroy all cluster munition remnants located in areas under its jurisdiction or control;

(d) Risk reduction education programmes and awareness activities to reduce the incidence of injuries or deaths caused by cluster munition remnants;

(e) Assistance to cluster munition victims; and

(f) The coordination relationship between the government of the State Party concerned and the relevant governmental, inter-governmental or non-governmental entities that will work in the implementation of the plan.

12. States Parties giving and receiving assistance under the provisions of this Article shall cooperate with a view to ensuring the full and prompt implementation of agreed assistance programmes.

Article 7

Transparency measures

1. Each State Party shall report to the Secretary-General of the United Nations as soon as practicable, and in any event not later than 180 days after the entry into force of this Convention for that State Party, on:

(a) The national implementation measures referred to in Article 9 of this Convention;

(b) The total of all cluster munitions, including explosive submunitions, referred to in paragraph 1 of Article 3 of this Convention, to include a breakdown of their type, quantity and, if possible, lot numbers of each type;

(c) The technical characteristics of each type of cluster muni-tion produced by that State Party prior to entry into force of this Convention for it, to the extent known, and those currently owned or possessed by it, giving, where reasonably possible, such categories of information as may facilitate identification and clearance of cluster munitions; at a

minimum, this information shall include the dimensions, fusing, explosive content, metallic content, colour photographs and other information that may facilitate the clearance of cluster munition remnants;

(d) The status and progress of programmes for the conversion or decommissioning of production facilities for cluster munitions;

(e) The status and progress of programmes for the destruction, in accordance with Article 3 of this Convention, of cluster munitions, including explosive submunitions, with details of the methods that will be used in destruction, the location of all destruction sites and the applicable safety and environmental standards to be observed;

(f) The types and quantities of cluster munitions, including explosive submunitions, destroyed in accordance with Article 3 of this Convention, including details of the methods of destruction used, the location of the destruction sites and the applicable safety and environmental standards observed;

(g) Stockpiles of cluster munitions, including explosive submunitions, discovered after reported completion of the programme referred to in sub-paragraph (e) of this paragraph, and plans for their destruction in accordance with Article 3 of this Convention;

(h) To the extent possible, the size and location of all cluster munition contaminated areas under its jurisdiction or control, to include as much detail as possible regarding the type and quantity of each type of cluster munition remnant in each such area and when they were used;

(i) The status and progress of programmes for the clearance and destruction of all types and quantities of cluster munition remnants cleared and destroyed in accordance with Article 4 of this Convention, to include the size and location of the cluster munition contaminated area cleared and a breakdown of the quantity of each type of cluster munition remnant cleared and destroyed;

(j) The measures taken to provide risk reduction education and, in particular, an immediate and effective warning to civilians living in cluster munition contaminated areas under its jurisdiction or control;

(k) The status and progress of implementation of its obligations under Article 5 of this Convention to adequately provide age- and gender- sensitive assistance, including medical care, rehabilitation and psychological support, as well as provide for social and economic inclusion of cluster munition victims and to collect reliable relevant data with respect to cluster munition victims;

(l) The name and contact details of the institutions mandated to provide information and to carry out the measures described in this paragraph;

(m) The amount of national resources, including financial, material or in kind, allocated to the implementation of Articles 3, 4 and 5 of this Convention; and

(n) The amounts, types and destinations of international cooperation and assistance provided under Article 6 of this Convention.

2. The information provided in accordance with paragraph 1 of this Article shall be updated by the States Parties annually, covering the previous calendar year, and

reported to the Secretary-General of the United Nations not later than 30 April of each year.

3. The Secretary-General of the United Nations shall transmit all such reports received to the States Parties.

Article 8
Facilitation and clarification of compliance

1. The States Parties agree to consult and cooperate with each other regarding the implementation of the provisions of this Convention and to work together in a spirit of cooperation to facilitate compliance by States Parties with their obligations under this Convention.

2. If one or more States Parties wish to clarify and seek to resolve questions relating to a matter of compliance with the provisions of this Convention by another State Party, it may submit, through the Secretary-General of the United Nations, a Request for Clarification of that matter to that State Party. Such a request shall be accompanied by all appropriate information. Each State Party shall refrain from unfounded Requests for Clarification, care being taken to avoid abuse. A State Party that receives a Request for Clarification shall provide, through the Secretary-General of the United Nations, within 28 days to the requesting State Party all information that would assist in clarifying the matter.

3. If the requesting State Party does not receive a response through the Secretary-General of the United Nations within that time period, or deems the response to the Request for Clarification to be unsatisfactory, it may submit the matter through the Secretary-General of the United Nations to the next Meeting of States Parties. The Secretary-General of the United Nations shall transmit the submission, accompanied by all appropriate information pertaining to the Request for Clarification, to all States Parties. All such information shall be presented to the requested State Party which shall have the right to respond.

4. Pending the convening of any Meeting of States Parties, any of the States Parties concerned may request the Secretary-General of the United Nations to exercise his or her good offices to facilitate the clarification requested.

5. Where a matter has been submitted to it pursuant to paragraph 3 of this Article, the Meeting of States Parties shall first determine whether to consider that matter further, taking into

account all information submitted by the States Parties concerned. If it does so determine, the Meeting of States Parties may suggest to the States Parties concerned ways and means further to clarify or resolve the matter under consideration, including the initiation of appropriate procedures in conformity with international law. In circumstances where the issue at hand is determined to be due to circumstances beyond the control of the requested State Party, the Meeting of States Parties may recommend appropriate measures, including the use of cooperative measures referred to in Article 6 of this Convention.

6. In addition to the procedures provided for in paragraphs 2 to 5 of this Article, the Meeting of States Parties may decide to adopt such other general procedures or specific mechanisms for clarification of compliance, including facts, and resolution of instances of non-compliance with the provisions of this Convention as it deems appropriate.

Article 9
National implementation measures

Each State Party shall take all appropriate legal, administrative and other measures to implement this Convention, including the imposition of penal sanctions to prevent and suppress any activity prohibited to a State Party under this Convention undertaken by persons or on territory under its jurisdiction or control.

Article 10
Settlement of disputes

1. When a dispute arises between two or more States Parties relating to the interpretation or application of this Convention, the States Parties concerned shall consult together with a view to the expeditious settlement of the dispute by negotiation or by other peaceful means of their choice, including recourse to the

Meeting of States Parties and referral to the International Court of Justice in conformity with the Statute of the Court.

2. The Meeting of States Parties may contribute to the settlement of the dispute by whatever means it deems appropriate, including offering its good offices, calling upon the States Parties concerned to start the settlement procedure of their choice and recommending a time-limit for any agreed procedure.

Article 11
Meetings of States Parties

1. The States Parties shall meet regularly in order to consider and, where necessary, take decisions in respect of any matter with regard to the application or implementation of this Convention, including:

(a) The operation and status of this Convention;

(b) Matters arising from the reports submitted under the provisions of this Convention;

(c) International cooperation and assistance in accordance with Article 6 of this Convention;

(d) The development of technologies to clear cluster munition remnants;

(e) Submissions of States Parties under Articles 8 and 10 of this Convention; and

(f) Submissions of States Parties as provided for in Articles 3 and 4 of this Convention.

2. The first Meeting of States Parties shall be convened by the Secretary-General of the United Nations within one year of entry into force of this Convention. The subsequent meetings shall be convened by the Secretary-General of the United Nations annually until the first Review Conference.

3. States not party to this Convention, as well as the United Nations, other relevant international organisations or institutions, regional organisations, the International Committee of the

Red Cross, the International Federation of Red Cross and Red Crescent Societies and relevant non-governmental organisations may be invited to attend these meetings as observers in accordance with the agreed rules of procedure.

Article 12
Review Conferences

1. A Review Conference shall be convened by the Secretary-General of the United Nations five years after the entry into force of this Convention. Further Review Conferences shall be convened by the Secretary-General of the United Nations if so requested by one or more States Parties, provided that the interval between Review Conferences shall in no case be less than five years. All States Parties to this Convention shall be invited to each Review Conference.

2. The purpose of the Review Conference shall be:

(a) To review the operation and status of this Convention;

(b) To consider the need for and the interval between further Meetings of States Parties referred to in paragraph 2 of Article 11 of this Convention; and

(c) To take decisions on submissions of States Parties as provided for in Articles 3 and 4 of this Convention.

3. States not party to this Convention, as well as the United Nations, other relevant international organisations or institutions, regional organisations, the International Committee of the Red Cross, the International Federation of Red Cross and Red Crescent Societies and relevant non-governmental organisations may be invited to attend each Review Conference as observers in accordance with the agreed rules of procedure.

Article 13
Amendments

1. At any time after its entry into force any State Party may propose amendments to this Convention. Any proposal for an amendment shall be communicated to the Secretary-General of the United Nations, who shall circulate it to all States Parties and shall seek their views on whether an Amendment Conference should be convened to consider the proposal. If a majority of the States Parties notify the Secretary-General of the United Nations no later than 90 days after its circulation that they support further consideration of the proposal, the Secretary-General of the United Nations shall convene an Amendment Conference to which all States Parties shall be invited.

2. States not party to this Convention, as well as the United Nations, other relevant international organisations or institutions, regional organisations, the International Committee of the Red Cross, the International Federation of Red Cross and Red Crescent Societies and relevant non-governmental organisations may be invited to attend each Amendment Conference as observers in accordance with the agreed rules of procedure.

3. The Amendment Conference shall be held immediately following a Meeting of States Parties or a Review Conference unless a majority of the States Parties request that it be held earlier.

4. Any amendment to this Convention shall be adopted by a majority of two-thirds of the States Parties present and voting at the Amendment Conference. The Depositary shall communicate any amendment so adopted to all States.

5. An amendment to this Convention shall enter into force for States Parties that have accepted the amendment on the date of deposit of acceptances by a majority of the States which were Parties at the date of adoption of the amendment. Thereafter it shall enter into force for any remaining State Party on the date of deposit of its instrument of acceptance.

Article 14

Costs and administrative tasks

1. The costs of the Meetings of States Parties, the Review Conferences and the Amendment Conferences shall be borne by the States Parties and States not party to this Convention participating therein, in accordance with the United Nations scale of assessment adjusted appropriately.

2. The costs incurred by the Secretary-General of the United Nations under Articles 7 and 8 of this Convention shall be borne by the States Parties in accordance with the United Nations scale of assessment adjusted appropriately.

3. The performance by the Secretary-General of the United Nations of administrative tasks assigned to him or her under this Convention is subject to an appropriate United Nations mandate.

Article 15
Signature

This Convention, done at Dublin on 30 May 2008, shall be open for signature at Oslo by all States on 3 December 2008 and thereafter at United Nations Headquarters in New York until its entry into force.

Article 16
Ratification, acceptance, approval or accession

1. This Convention is subject to ratification, acceptance or approval by the Signatories.

2. It shall be open for accession by any State that has not signed the Convention.

3. The instruments of ratification, acceptance, approval or accession shall be deposited with the Depositary.

Article 17

Entry into force

1. This Convention shall enter into force on the first day of the sixth month after the month in which the thirtieth instrument of ratification, acceptance, approval or accession has been deposited.

2. For any State that deposits its instrument of ratification, acceptance, approval or accession after the date of the deposit of the thirtieth instrument of ratification, acceptance, approval or accession, this Convention shall enter into force on the first day of the sixth month after the date on which that State has deposited its instrument of ratification, acceptance, approval or accession.

Article 18
Provisional application

Any State may, at the time of its ratification, acceptance, approval or accession, declare that it will apply provisionally Article 1 of this Convention pending its entry into force for that State.

Article 19
Reservations

The Articles of this Convention shall not be subject to reservations.

Article 20
Duration and withdrawal

1. This Convention shall be of unlimited duration.

2. Each State Party shall, in exercising its national sovereignty, have the right to withdraw from this Convention. It shall give notice of such withdrawal to all other States Parties, to the Depositary and to the United Nations Security Council. Such

instrument of withdrawal shall include a full explanation of the reasons motivating withdrawal.

3. Such withdrawal shall only take effect six months after the receipt of the instrument of withdrawal by the Depositary. If, however, on the expiry of that six-month period, the withdrawing State Party is engaged in an armed conflict, the withdrawal shall not take effect before the end of the armed conflict.

Article 21

Relations with States not party to this Convention

1. Each State Party shall encourage States not party to this Convention to ratify, accept, approve or accede to this Convention, with the goal of attracting the adherence of all States to this Convention.

2. Each State Party shall notify the governments of all States not party to this Convention, referred to in paragraph 3 of this Article, of its obligations under this

Convention, shall promote the norms it establishes and shall make its best efforts to discourage States not party to this Convention from using cluster munitions.

3. Notwithstanding the provisions of Article 1 of this Convention and in accordance with international law, States Parties, their military personnel or nationals, may engage in military cooperation and operations with States not party to this Convention that might engage in activities prohibited to a State Party.

4. Nothing in paragraph 3 of this Article shall authorise a State Party:

(a) To develop, produce or otherwise acquire cluster munitions;

(b) To itself stockpile or transfer cluster munitions;

(c) To itself use cluster munitions; or

(d) To expressly request the use of cluster munitions in cases where the choice of munitions used is within its exclusive control.

Article 22
Depositary

The Secretary-General of the United Nations is hereby designated as the Depositary of this Convention.

Article 23
Authentic texts

The Arabic, Chinese, English, French, Russian and Spanish texts of this Convention shall be equally authentic.

ACKNOWLEDGMENTS

I would like to thank all those who supported me in writing this book, both this revised edition and the first one, published two years earlier. I especially want to thank my parents, Ashish and Ratna Mukherjee, whose support and encouragement helped me every step of the way. They listened to me complain, helped me brainstorm ideas in the middle of the night, and put up with me when I was grumpy and cranky, which was more often than I care to admit.

This book is based on my Master's thesis, and I want to especially thank the following professors at Cornell who helped shape my work and give me direction during that time: Professor David Lewis, the late Professor Emeritus Jerome Zeigler, Professor Norman Uphoff, Professor Nancy Chau, Assistant Professor Asif Efrat and Professor Pete Loucks. I also want to thank Jeff Abramson and Firoz Alizada of the Cluster Munition Coalition for taking the time to answer questions for the book. This book would also not be possible without the tremendous amount of research and extensive publications made available by various organizations, NGOs and other research bodies. Lastly, I want to thank all those who I have worked with on various projects related to human rights and international law, too numerous to mention here, who have helped shape my understanding and worldview of international relations and human rights law.

ABOUT THE AUTHOR

Geetanjali Mukherjee grew up in India, spending her early years in Kolkata, and then attending high school in New Delhi. She went on to read law as an undergraduate at the University of Warwick, United Kingdom, where she joined as many clubs as possible while still giving the impression she understood the intricacies of trusts law. She went on to earn a Masters' in Public Administration from Cornell University, United States, while trying not to freeze along with the famed Ithaca lakes. She is also a member of Pi Alpha Alpha, the Global Honor Society for Public Affairs and Administration.

Geetanjali is the author of twelve books, although sometimes it feels like the one she is writing is the very first one. She currently lives in Singapore.

She loves to hear from readers, so please get in touch on social media or send her an email: geetanjalimukherjee. author@gmail.com

If you liked the book and have a spare moment, I would really appreciate a short review on the retailer page. Your help in spreading the word is gratefully appreciated as reviews make a huge difference to helping new readers find the book. Thank you!

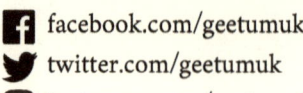

facebook.com/geetumuk
twitter.com/geetumuk
instagram.com/geetumuk